English Language Teaching

Approaches, Methods, Techniques

THIRD EDITION

Geetha Nagaraj

Orient BlackSwan

ENGLISH LANGUAGE TEACHING: APPROACHES, METHODS, TECHNIQUES

ORIENT BLACKSWAN PRIVATE LIMITED

Registered office
3-6-752 Himayatnagar, Hyderabad 500 029, Telangana, India
E-mail: centraloffice@orientblackswan.com

Other offices
Bengaluru, Chennai, Guwahati, Hyderabad, Kolkata,
Mumbai, New Delhi, Noida, Patna, Visakhapatnam

First published by Orient Longman Private Limited 1996
Reprinted 2000, 2001, 2003, 2004, 2005, 2006
Second edition 2008
First Orient Blackswan impression 2010
Reprinted 2012, 2013
Third edition 2021

033656

ISBN 978 93 5442 078 8

Typeset in Adobe Garamond Pro 11/13 *by*
DiTech Publishing Services Private Limited, Faridabad 121 002

Printed at
Glorious Printers, Delhi 110 095

Published by
Orient Blackswan Private Limited
3-6-752 Himayatnagar, Hyderabad 500 029, Telangana, India
E-mail: info@orientblackswan.com

Contents

Part II TECHNIQUES

Acknowledgements

The author wishes to acknowledge her indebtedness to Professor T.R. Keshav Rao, who contributed substantially to the preparation of the chapters on the grammar-translation method, the S-O-S approach and the communicational syllabus.

The publishers acknowledge the use of copyrighted materials taken from the following sources:

- Excerpts from W.M. Rivers, *Teaching Foreign-Language Skills*. Chicago: The University of Chicago Press, 1968. Republished by permission of University of Chicago Press; permission conveyed through Copyright Clearance Center, Inc.
- M.S. Patel, 'The Structural Syllabus at Work in India', *ELT Journal*, 1962, vol. 16, issue no. 3, pp. 145–51. Reproduced by permission of Oxford University Press.
- Excerpts from V.F. Allen, *Techniques in Teaching Vocabulary*. Copyright © Oxford University Press, 1983. Reproduced by permission of Oxford University Press.
- 'IELTS band descriptors' and 'The IELTS Scale' material from the table titled 'Writing Task 1: Band Descriptors' (Scale Material) from www.ielts.org. Reproduced by permission of IELTS Australia and International Development Program (IDP).
- 'Skill-getting and skill-using' chart from Wilga M. Rivers and Mary S. Temperley, *A Practical Guide to the Teaching of English as a Second or Foreign Language*. Copyright © 1978 by Oxford University Press, Inc. Reproduced by permission of the licensor through PLSclear.

- Illustrations from Chris Culshaw and Deborah Waters, *Headwork, Book 4*, Oxford University Press 1984. Copyright © 1984 by Oxford University Press. Reproduced by permission of the licensor through PLSclear.

The icons used for sections within the chapters are from the following sources:

- THINK IT OVER: 'Settings', icon made by srip, from www.flaticon.com.
- CHAPTER/SECTION SUMMARY: 'Register', icon made by Pixel perfect, from www.flaticon.com.
- DID YOU UNDERSTAND?: 'Light bulb', icon made by Pixel perfect, from www.flaticon.com.
- APPLICATION: 'Jigsaw', icon made by srip, from www.flaticon.com.
- FURTHER READING: 'Book', icon made by Freepik, from www.flaticon.com.

Every attempt has been made to contact holders of copyright. Where the publishers have not heard from them at the time of going to press or where, in the absence of complete information, it has not been possible to identify the sources of materials used, they would be glad to hear from the copyright holders concerned to enable them to make appropriate acknowledgement in future editions of this book.

Preface to the Third Edition

In the thirteen years since the publication of the second edition, the field of English language teaching has seen interesting changes in the ways in which language is taught and learnt. Advances in technology—especially high-speed internet and all that it enables us to now do—has encouraged bottom–up student-centred approaches and made remote learning simpler. Access to authentic resources (the way language is used in everyday speech and writing) has become widespread. Classrooms have steadily become more diverse as well.

However, some things remain unchanged. Most of the principles underlying teaching and assessment still hold true. Time-tested techniques of instruction and evaluation are just as effective today as they were when this book was first written. And English has, if anything, cemented its role as the lingua franca of science, technology, business, media, and corporate communication.

This revised edition of *English Language Teaching: Approaches, Methods, Techniques* updates the chapter on teaching aids to reflect the increased use of digital tools and platforms. Many smaller improvements and corrections have been made throughout the book. I hope this new edition will help teachers keep pace with the evolving nature of language teaching, while giving them a firm grounding in all that continues to stay relevant.

Geetha Nagaraj

Preface to the First Edition

> The difference between education and training lies solely in the coercion which training claims as its right. Training is forcible education. Education is free.
>
> Tolstoy 1862

The aim of this book on English language teaching (ELT) methodology is simple: it wants to educate teacher-participants/teachers about ELT, not train them in it. All informed modern thinking is against lockstep training of teachers. A teacher/teacher-to-be is a thinking human being, and her/his full potential can be reached only if she/he is encouraged to think and develop as an individual and a professional. Like descriptive grammar, this book only describes. Teachers have to make the final choice about what they do and how they want to do it.

Writing about the essential nature of the relationship between teachers and students, Freire (1972) says:

> A careful analysis of the teacher–student relationship at any level, inside or outside the school, reveals its fundamentally narrative character. The relationship involves a narrating subject (the teacher) and patient, listening objects (the students) .... Education is suffering from narration sickness.

This book attempts a cure for 'narration sickness' by inviting users to participate in the learning process.

THINK IT OVER means exactly what it says—after reading a section, readers are asked to think over, discuss and perhaps argue over the points mentioned. The statements and questions in this section are sometimes provocative and sometimes heavily biased—all of which has been done to start the critical process functioning. No task is set as this section does not aim to find out how much thinking has gone on in quantifiable terms, but to engender a qualitative change.

Under APPLICATION are practical tasks set to make readers apply their critical reasoning to real situations as they exist in the field. Till one prepares a passage for a structural reader, one is not fully aware of the process which preparing such readers involves. It is hoped that this section in every chapter will be taken seriously and exploited fully.

The FURTHER READING section puts readers in touch with thoughts, ideas and opinions of prominent personalities in the field of ELT. The articles/excerpts are not always laudatory—they raise questions, express honest doubts and voice criticisms, all of which happen when one is productively critical. Many such doubts and questions have been the basis of revolutionary methodologies. The search for the 'perfect method', which is as elusive as the Holy Grail, is still going on.

A short GLOSSARY OF ELT TERMS has been included for easy reference.

We hope you enjoy reading this book and doing the tasks, for no real learning can take place without enjoyment.

Geetha Nagaraj

English in the World

'An international language belongs to its users, not to the countries whose national languages have become internationalised' (Edge 1993). The position of English in the world has changed so greatly and the number of second-language (L2) speakers has increased so rapidly that all the descriptions of the place of English among world languages need to be rewritten.

Background

For quite a few decades, English was taught and learnt with the educated native speaker as a model. The two accepted varieties were British and American English. English language learning was an effort directed at reaching as close an approximation of the native speaker model as possible.

After the dissolution of the colonies and the gaining of independence of the once colonised nations, English did not, as expected, disappear. It started developing as a means of communication in multilingual as well as near-monolingual communities, happily taking on the cultural and linguistic nuances of the speech communities that were using this language. Thus, you had the 'small-small pieces' of Sri Lankan English and the Indian kinship term 'cousin sister' making the relationship clear.

Economic and technological forces played their part in keeping English at the centre of communication. The United States of America emerged as the leader in computer technology, and English, by default, was the language it operated in. So, instead of remaining a quaint relic of colonialism, English succeeded in re-inventing itself as the language of global communication.

Kachru (1985) divides English in the world into three circles: the inner circle consisting of 'native' speakers for whom English is the first and often only language; the outer circle of people using English as a second language for official and inter-state as well as international communication; and the expanding circle of speakers learning English as a foreign language, generally for specific purposes. If we take Crystal's (1997) estimate of the number of speakers of English in each category, we get the following:

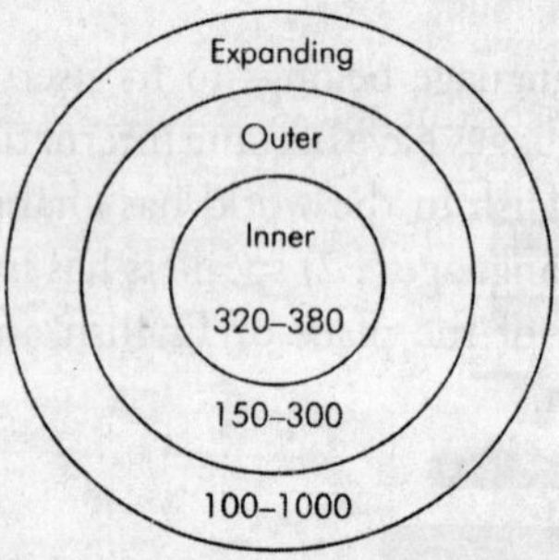

The three circles of English according to Kachru (1985), with estimates of speaker numbers in millions according to Crystal (1997)

English in the world today

In 2000, the British Council published a detailed study of the English language in the world. Graddol (1997) looks at a range of quantifiable data about the English language, and tries to make an informed and objective forecast of the position of English in the world's fast-changing social and economic spheres. Whatever be the future of English, figures show that it is way ahead of other languages when it comes to communication across continents and peoples. The figures below confirm the fact.

The language of home pages on the web (c. 1997)

	Language	Estimated servers	%
1	English	332,778	84.3
2	German	17,971	4.5
3	Japanese	12,348	3.1

4	French	7,213	1.8
5	Spanish	4,646	1.2
6	Swedish	4,279	1.1
7	Italian	3,790	1.0
8	Portuguese	2,567	0.7
9	Dutch	2,445	0.6
10	Norwegian	2,323	0.6

Inter-continental telephone traffic (1994)

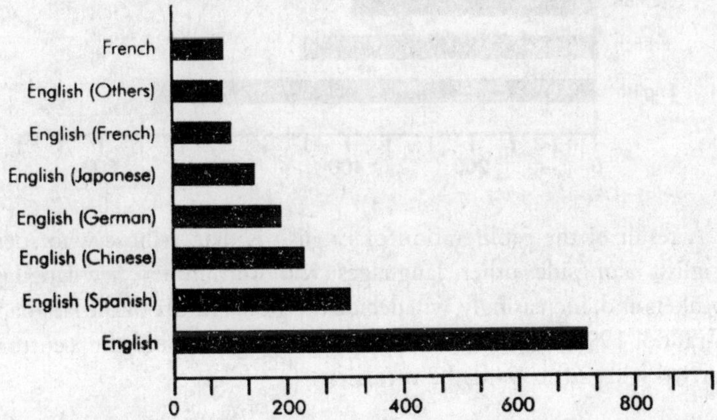

Proportion of books published in different languages (early 1990s)

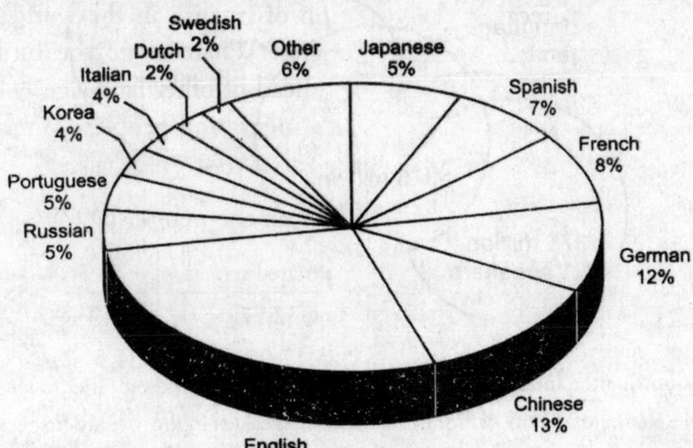

Language engineering products available for major languages in the mid-1990s

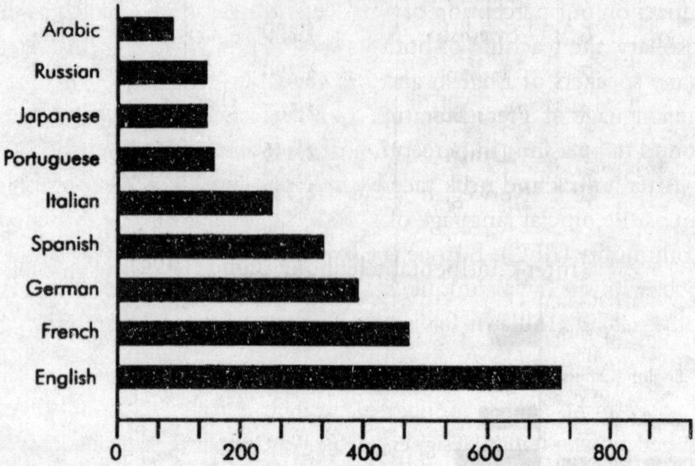

A result of the proliferation of English is that '[t]hose who speak English alongside other languages will outnumber first-language speakers and, increasingly, will decide the global future of the language' (Graddol 1997). Kachru's three circles will overlap and the 'centre of gravity' will shift towards L2 speakers.

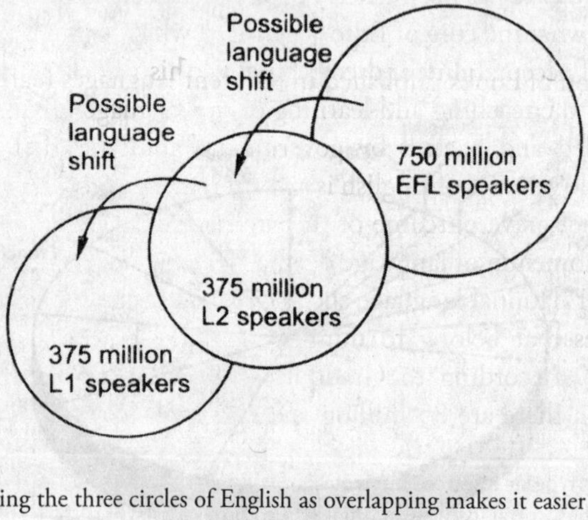

Showing the three circles of English as overlapping makes it easier to see how the 'centre of gravity' will shift towards L2 speakers in the twenty-first century.

Implications

The implications of the use of English in the world today will have an impact on our perception of what constitutes 'good' English and, as a corollary, the teaching of both its spoken and written forms. With so many speakers of English and the change in its function from being the language of 'great literature' to a tool of communication, there is bound to be a shift in perception of what acceptable English is.

After a neck and neck race with German and French, English won out as the official language of transaction of the European Economic Community (EEC). Europe is a continent with a variety of languages, each with its own unique set of features. Therefore, as in many countries like India, it has many brands of English. Here is what the *Guardian Weekly* (19 April 2001) had to say:

> A Finnish scientist coming to Vienna for a conference on human genetics; an Italian designer negotiating with prospective clients in Stockholm; a Polish tourist chatting with restaurateurs in Crete; they all communicate successfully in 'English', but which 'English'? Well, chances are that it is not the language you hear in chat shows and soaps on British or American television, but rather a range of 'Englishes', with enough of a common core so as to make it viable as a means of communication.

An initiative has been taken to conduct research that will ultimately describe what the core of Euro-English is, which will ultimately define norms of acceptability and correctness.[1] This will, of course, have an effect on the teaching and learning of the language. That such studies are funded and backed by governments indicates that the idea of acceptable varieties of English is a norm rather than an exception today.

Another grave outcome of the proliferation of a single language is the phenomenon of language death. The language could be English or any other national language such as Bahasa Indonesia, to which other languages that belong to minority and less-powerful groups could succumb. According to Graddol (1997), it is feared that Javanese (of which there are 85 million speakers) will be swamped by Bahasa

[1] A similar type of research, but not on the same scale, was undertaken by Professor Bansal of the Central Institute of English and Foreign Languages (CIEFL) with regard to the intelligibility of Indian English. The research focused on features of pronunciation, and not on pronunciation and lexicogrammar as in the European study.

Indonesia, the national language. Campaigns have been launched in the UK to keep the Cornish language alive. Since English is a highly visible language in the world today, it is often seen as the villain of the piece, responsible for the waning and death of many local languages.

Where English will go from here is anybody's guess. It is a time of exciting changes in its development; the changes are occurring much faster than at any other time in the history of the English language. As teachers of English, we need to be aware of the changes and sensitive to the setting of norms.

THINK IT OVER

What features of English, do you think, have made it acceptable to different speech communities in the world?

Part I

We shall begin with some important methodologies which have vitally influenced teaching and materials production as they gradually evolved over the years.

The chapters in this part are arranged in chronological order.

1

The Grammar-Translation Method

Brief history

> No full and carefully documented history of grammar translation exists.
>
> Stern 1983

The grammar-translation method cannot probably be traced back to the tenets of any particular master teacher or methodologist, but it seems to be rooted in the formal teaching of Greek and Latin which prevailed in Europe for many centuries. Though Latin and Greek were not learnt for communication, they were considered to be useful for intellectual discipline and were seen as prestige symbols.

The grammar-translation method was a product of German scholarship. It was known in the United States of America as the 'Prussian method' as it had its origin in Germany—or to be more exact, in Prussia—at the end of the eighteenth century. Some of its leading exponents were J. Seidenstucker, Karl Plotz, H.G. Ollendorff and J.V. Meidinger—all German scholars. This method was widely used in European and foreign-language teaching from the 1840s to the 1940s, and in a slightly modified form it is used in some parts of the world even today.

The earliest grammar-translation course for the teaching of English was written in 1793 by J.C. Fick and published in South Germany. It was modelled on a book for the teaching of French by the originator of the method, J.V. Meidinger, and was called *A Practical Course in English for Germans*. The word 'practical' here meant 'for practice', and it was not used in the modern sense of the word 'for use'. The book contained exercises of various kinds, particularly exercises for translating sentences into and out of the foreign language. A lot of importance was attached to completeness of sentences and accuracy. There was an utter neglect of the spoken language.

What is the grammar-translation method?

It is a way of learning a language through a detailed study of its grammar. The learner then applies the rules of grammar in translating sentences and parts of texts from the mother tongue into the target language and vice versa.

> The first language is maintained as the reference system in the acquisition of the second language.
>
> Stern 1983

The following is a list of the features of the method:

- Grammar is taught prescriptively—through the presentation and study of rules.
- Practice is provided through translation exercises from the mother tongue to the target language and vice versa.
- A distinctive feature of this method is its focus on translating the sentence.
- Accuracy is given great importance. The learner is required to attain high standards in translation. A.P.R. Howatt (1984) says: 'High priority is attached to meticulous standards of accuracy which, as well as having an intrinsic moral value, was a prerequisite for passing the increasing number of formal written examinations that grew up during the nineteenth century.'
- Vocabulary is taught through bilingual word lists, reference to dictionaries, and memorisation of words and their meanings.
- The method focuses primarily on the skills of reading and writing, with little emphasis on listening or speaking.
- The mother tongue of the learner is used to explain new items and make comparisons with their equivalents in the target language.

Think it over

1. Have you learnt a language through this method?
2. Do you know if there are any languages that are taught like this today?

Syllabus

The syllabus consists of the following:

- eight to ten prose lessons of specified limits
- seven to eight poems
- a non-detailed text, usually an abridged classic
- grammar
  a. parts of speech, including their definitions and articles
  b. conjugation of verbs in the affirmative, negative, interrogative and negative interrogative
  c. parsing of words in different types of sentences
  d. passivisation
  e. reported speech comprising reporting statements and questions
  f. analysis of simple, complex and compound sentences
  g. synthesis of sentences
- written work
  a. descriptive writing
  b. narrative writing
  c. letters of different kinds

Texts

Most of the texts at the secondary level were written by scholars who were not engaged in teaching at the secondary level. The texts usually contained long extracts from the works of great writers, chosen for their intellectual content rather than for their linguistic value, without taking the learner's interests into consideration. The textbooks also consisted of long vocabulary lists—sometimes bilingual—as well as written exercises, especially translation exercises.

The main concern of the teacher was to cover all the lessons in the book in a given period of time. She/he would first read the given passage, and would then explain its content and the meanings of new words in the mother tongue. Rules of grammar were taught elaborately, followed by practice in writing paradigms.

> Texts in the foreign language are translated into the native language orally and in writing and, ideally, their literary and cultural significance

is discussed, although in many classes, because of the limitation in the time available, this is done very perfunctorily, if at all.

Rivers 1968

In this method, the teacher is totally dependent on the *text* as she/he follows the given lessons and exercises in it rigidly. She/he has little scope for innovative planning required to incorporate the actual needs of the learner in the classroom. The learner is therefore exposed only to literary language. Communication skills are neglected, with little attention to correct pronunciation. The learner does *not* play an active role in the use of the target language. His/her role is rather passive.

In the classroom—a simulation

The input, given below, is taken from George Orwell's *Decline of the English Murder and Other Essays*. George Orwell served in the Imperial Police in Burma during the 1920s. Below is an account of a hanging he witnessed.

It was in Burma, a sodden morning of the rains. A sickly light, like yellow tinfoil, was slanting over the high walls in to the jail yard. We were waiting outside the condemned cells, a row of sheds fronted with double bars, like small animal cages. Each cell measured about ten feet by ten and was quite bare within except for a plank bed and a pot for drinking water. In some of them brown, silent men were squatting at the inner bars, with their blankets draped round them. These were the condemned men, due to be hanged within the next week or two.

Step 1 Learners read the passage.

Teacher	Nimish, read the next two lines.
Learner	Each cell measured about ten feet by ten and was quite bare within except for a plank bed and a pot for drinking water.
Teacher	Now translate the sentence.
Learner	(in mother tongue) What does 'cell' mean?
Teacher	(Gives translation in mother tongue.)
Learner	(Translates.)
Teacher	(Helps with 'except for' and 'measured'.)

This activity continues till the passage is done.

Step 2

Teacher	Any questions?
Learner	What does 'sodden' mean?
Teacher	(Translates into the mother tongue. Gives explanations and illustrations in the mother tongue.)
Learner	(in mother tongue) What is the meaning of 'fronted with double bars'?
Teacher	(Gives a corresponding phrase in the mother tongue.)

Step 3

Teacher	Now let's do the questions. Radhika and Kamal, begin with the first question.
Learner 1	What sort of a morning was it?
Learner 2	It was a sodden morning.

Learners work out all the questions. The answers given by the learners are checked by the teacher for correctness.

Step 4 The next activity involves vocabulary work.

Teacher	Look at the list of words given. Can you give words in your mother tongues for these? [Sodden, cells, condemned, cages.]

Learners give the mother tongue equivalents. The teacher helps if necessary.

Teacher	Look at the next list of words. Each of them has a word with the opposite meaning in the text. Find them. [Crowded, big, low, dry.]

Step 5 The next part of the lesson deals with the teaching of grammar deductively.

Teacher	A noun is a name. It may be the name of a person like 'Mary', or of a place like 'Delhi'. These nouns are proper nouns. They begin with a capital letter. A noun can also be the name of something we can see or touch, such as 'table' or 'pot'. These are concrete nouns. There are other nouns that we can neither touch nor see, for example 'truth', 'beauty' and 'honour'. These are abstract nouns.

Collective nouns refer to groups, such as 'team', crowd', 'committee'.

- From the first paragraph of the passage find three things that can be found in the cell.
- What kind of nouns are these?
- What kind of noun is 'Burma'?
- Most nouns form their plural by adding an 's'. Find two nouns from the first paragraph which form the plural in this way.
- There is one noun in the passage which does not form the plural by adding an 's'. Find it.

Step 6 The next part is an exercise.

Teacher Identify the nouns in the following sentences and say whether they are concrete, abstract or collective nouns.

- The crowd was very big.
- We all love honesty.
- He gave me some grapes.
- Our team is better than theirs.
- Solomon was famous for his wisdom.

Think it over

1. Do you think that all the practices of the grammar-translation method are useless? Why or why not? (In thinking about this, you could perhaps consider the fact that it was practised for a long time.)
2. What features of the grammar-translation method do we still retain in a lot of our teaching?

Chapter summary

- The grammar-translation method had its origin in Germany and was popular from the 1840s to the 1940s.
- It is a way of learning a language by studying the rules of its grammar and then applying these rules to the translation of sentences and texts.

- Vocabulary is taught through bilingual word lists.
- Accuracy of language is given great importance.
- The method focuses primarily on reading and writing skills, with little attention to listening and speaking.
- The syllabus comprises prose, poetry, grammar and written work.
- The texts consist of long extracts from the works of great writers, chosen for their intellectual content.
- The method is not too demanding on the teacher.

DID YOU UNDERSTAND?

1. What are the main features of the grammar-translation method?
2. 'Grammar is taught prescriptively.' What do you understand by the term 'prescriptively'? Can you give an example of how grammar can be taught prescriptively?
3. What sort of a syllabus did the grammar-translation method follow? What was the focus of the syllabus?
4. Why was writing included in the syllabus?
5. Compare the syllabus for teaching Sanskrit in schools with the syllabus and methodology of the grammar-translation method. Are there any similarities? List them.

APPLICATION

Teach the following lesson to any class you deem fit using the grammar-translation method. A few tasks have been suggested for use.

Doctor Goldsmith's medicine

One day a poor woman called at his house and asked him if he would come to see her husband who was sick and would not eat any food. When Goldsmith called on the family, he found that they were very poor because the man had no work for a considerable time.

He discovered that there was no food in the house.

'Come and see me this evening', said Goldsmith to the wife, 'and I will let you have some medicine for your husband.'

When the woman called that evening Goldsmith gave her a small box which was quite heavy for its size.

'This is the medicine', he exclaimed. 'See that it is properly used and it will do your husband a world of good. But please do not open the box until you get home.'

'What are the directions for taking it?' asked the woman.

'You will find full directions inside the box', he replied.

Immediately on reaching home the woman sat down beside her husband and opened the box very carefully. It was full of money, on top of which was a slip of paper bearing the words:

'To be taken as often as necessity requires.'

Once again Oliver Goldsmith had given away his money to help the poor.

Richards 1981

Task 1

Write the mother tongue equivalents (meanings) of the following words and phrases used in the text.

a. immediately
b. called at
c. called on
d. considerable
e. discovered
f. a world of good
g. directions
h. necessity

Task 2

Translate the following sentences from the text into the mother tongue.

a. He discovered that there was no food in the house.
b. The man had no work for a considerable time.
c. I will let you have some medicine for your husband.
d. What are the directions for taking it?
e. To be taken as often as necessity requires.

Task 3

a. Analyse the following sentence into clauses and show their relationship with the main clause:
'Oliver Goldsmith, who was called Dr Goldsmith because he had studied medicine, gave away so much to the poor that he had little money left for himself.'
b. Say whether it is a complex sentence or a compound sentence.
c. Pick out similar sentences from the text and ask the learner to analyse them. Use the mother tongue for explanation.

Task 4

a. Change the following into reported speech: 'Come and see me this evening', said Goldsmith to the wife, 'and I will let you have some medicine for your husband.'
b. Pick out similar sentences in direct speech and ask the learner to change them into reported speech. Use the mother tongue to explain the changes to be effected.

Task 5

Choose a few sentences in the mother tongue pertaining to the story and ask the learners to translate them into English.

Task 6

Ask comprehension questions to check learners' comprehension of the story.

Further reading

Teaching foreign-language skills

He takes a seat out of the view of the students and opens his notepad. In the rows before him the students are opening their foreign-language textbooks and preparing for the day's lesson. They are about to begin a new section. Before them on the page is a reading selection with, above it, two or three long columns of new vocabulary items with native-language equivalents. These the students have been asked to learn by heart the night before. As this memorisation is a rather boring chore, some of the students are hastily babbling over to themselves some of the words they have not yet learned. The lesson begins with a quick written test of these new words. Students, when asked to give their answers, spell out the foreign-language words letter by letter in their native language, because they feel shy and uncertain about pronouncing them in front of their classmates. The teacher is not very satisfied with the result of this test, but the work for the day must be covered, so he moves on. The students are asked to read out in the foreign language the selection in the book before them. One after another they stumble through the sentences. After a while this reading around the class is omitted because the procedure is too painful for the teacher and too embarrassing for the students. For a few sentences the teacher reads the passage aloud to the class himself. Then the students are asked to look over the rest of the passage silently, because the reading-aloud process seems rather wasteful of class time for the little it achieves.

Then begins the process of translation. One after another students translate the sentences of the passage into their native language, with occasional help from the teacher. Things are progressing well: the teacher can now pass on to what he feels is the real business of the day. On the chalkboard, he sets out what he considers to be a lucid outline of the use of the past tense, examples of which have been artificially and cunningly worked into the reading passage. He warms to his task, explaining in great detail in the native language the traditional rules for the use of this particular tense in all the logically passive situations. Where these explanations involve terminology with which the students are presumed not to be familiar, he takes some time to teach this terminology as it applies to the grammar of the native language and then applies it to the foreign language.

The students copy into their books various rules, examples and what seem to them to be even more numerous exceptions. The teacher asks a few questions. When the students appear to have grasped the point of the grammatical exposition they settle down to spend the rest of the lesson on the not-too-demanding task of writing out paradigms and filling in blanks in grammatical exercises, or they translate from the native language into the foreign language sentences in which the past tense is required. For this latter exercise the students are presented with sentences which have been artificially constructed to include all possible aspects of the rules being studied. Many of these sentences are very unlikely to be of any real value to the students who frequently distort the original meaning as they try to construct their own version of the foreign language. Exercises the students have not finished and the learning of rules and paradigms are assigned for home study, with the extra spice of a few irregular verbs and some more vocabulary items.

Rivers 1968

2

The Structural-Oral-Situational Approach

Brief history

The structural-oral-situational approach, popularly known as the S-O-S approach, came into being as an alternative to the direct method[1] of teaching English as a second language. The 'structural approach' is an outcome of the experiments carried out in language teaching in army camps during World War II. The entry of the United States of America into the war had a significant effect on language teaching in America. The American government needed personnel who were fluent in German, French, Italian, Chinese, Japanese and other languages, and who could work as interpreters, code-room assistants and translators. It became, therefore, necessary to set up a special language-training programme. The government wanted American universities to develop foreign-language programmes for military personnel. Thus the Army Specialized Training Program (ASTP) was established in 1942. By the beginning of 1943, fifty-five American universities were involved in the programme. The ASTP lasted only about two years but made a considerable impact on the academic community, linguists and language teachers. Linguists and applied linguists during this period were becoming increasingly involved in the teaching of English as a foreign language. The demand for foreign expertise in the teaching of English was growing. Thousands of students from foreign countries who came to America for higher studies required training in English before they could begin their studies. These factors led to the emergence of what is popularly known as the S-O-S approach in the mid-fifties.

[1] See Chapter 5, 'Other Methods', p. 70.

In 1941, the University of Michigan established the first English language institute in the USA. The primary aim of the institute was to train teachers of English to teach English as a foreign language or as a second language. Charles Fries, the director of the institute, had training in structural linguistics, and he applied its principles to language teaching. Fries and his colleagues were not happy with the direct method of teaching English, in which the learners were exposed to the whole body of the language to begin with, and then expected to gradually absorb its grammatical patterns. For Fries, grammar, or *structure*, was the starting point in teaching language. The structure of English was identified with its basic sentence patterns and grammatical structures. Language was taught by intensive oral drilling of the basic sentence patterns. Systematic attention was paid to pronunciation. Teaching techniques concentrated on repetition of a pattern a number of times so that the learner became perfect in the use of the pattern. Systematic courses and materials were developed based on important patterns to teach English as a second language. Besides the University of Michigan, a number of other universities also developed similar programmes. In 1950, the American Council of Learned Societies was commissioned to develop textbooks for teaching English to speakers of a number of foreign languages.

While the structural approach developed by linguists at Michigan and other universities was gaining ground, applied linguists and methodologists in Britain were developing the 'oral approach' to teaching English as a foreign/second language. The two traditions developed independently. Two prominent linguists in this movement were Harold Palmer and A.S. Hornby. They developed a more scientific foundation for the oral approach than was seen in the direct method, and, by the 1950s, the oral approach was the accepted British approach to English language teaching. It is described in the standard methodology textbooks of the period such as those of F.G. French (1948–50), P. Gurrey (1955), A.W. Frisby (1957) and F.L. Billows (1961).

It was Hornby himself who used the term 'situational approach' in the title of a popular series of articles published in *ELT* (1950). The approach suggests that any language item, whether it be a structure or a word, should not be presented in isolation. It has to be introduced and practised in a context, situationally.

From the historical details given above it can be seen that the structural-oral-situational approach became very effective in teaching English as a foreign/second language in the late 1940s and early 1950s.

It was in 1952 that the S-O-S approach made its advent in India. Madras (present-day Tamil Nadu) was the first state in India to agree to use the S-O-S approach for the teaching of English as second language. Jean Forester, the principal of a teacher-training college in Chennai, was in charge of the programme. Very soon, the British Council took interest in popularising the approach. ELT experts from England helped the Madras government in framing the syllabus and producing relevant materials. The Madras English Language Teaching (MELT) campaign was started to provide training to all the teachers of English in the new approach. The training programme used the snowball effect[2] for the propagation of the new approach. Madras had a number of nodal centres in important cities which trained the resource persons, who, in turn, trained the practising teachers. An effective follow-up programme was also prepared to meet the needs of English teachers and guide them in classrooms. The British Council also sent Indian ELT experts from Madras to various English universities for further training in English language teaching.

The S-O-S approach to the teaching of English became so effective in Madras that the other southern states of India wanted the approach to be introduced in their states too. As a result of this, it was thought that instead of starting separate English language teaching institutes in each of the southern states, it would be better to have one institute in the south which could train the English teachers from the (then) four southern states and also produce for them syllabuses, materials and textbooks based on the S-O-S approach. This led to the starting of the Regional Institute of English at Bangalore in 1963. The institute has since been training teachers of English from southern India, and also helping to produce materials and texts for the states.

What is the structural-oral-situational approach?

The S-O-S approach is the presentation and practice of carefully selected and graded grammatical structures of English in effective, meaningful situations, initially through speech and later through reading and

[2] to grow bigger at a faster and faster rate, like a snowball rolling down a mountainside

writing. Language is viewed as structurally related elements for the encoding of meaning—the elements being phonemes, morphemes, words, structures and sentence types. It can be diagrammatically represented as follows.

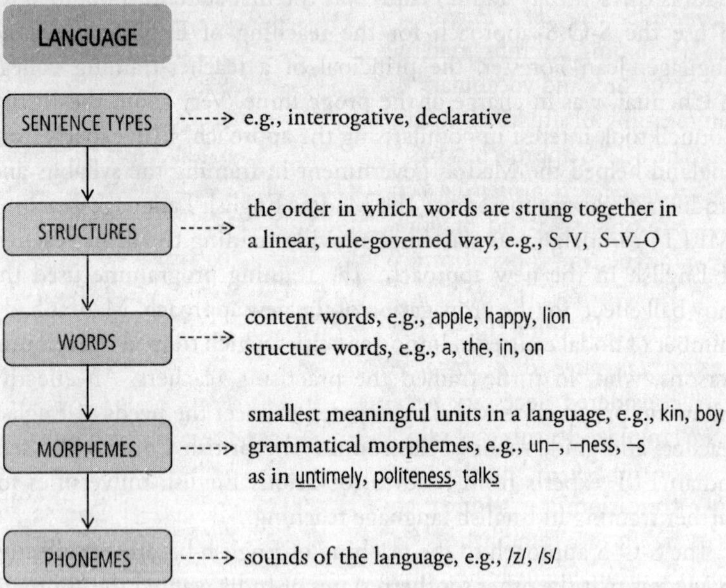

Structures, or teaching items, are selected and graded by language teaching experts and methodologists. 'Grading' is a term used for ordering the language items according to what comes before what, and what goes with what. It means that 'we cannot start anywhere or with anything; for in a system one thing fits into another, and one thing depends on another' (Mackey 1965).

For the purpose of grading the structures, the following criteria are taken into account:

- whether the items are frequently used by the users of the language
- whether the items are useful for the purposes of learning the language
- whether the items can be easily taught and learnt
- which items can be grouped together for the purpose of teaching

Similarly, vocabulary items are also selected and graded. Frequency counts of the basic vocabulary used in English show that a core of two thousand words or so occurs frequently in written texts and these words greatly help the learner in learning a foreign language. Harold Palmer, Michael West and other specialists produced a guide to the English vocabulary needed for teaching English as a foreign language. This was later revised by Michael West and published in 1953 as *A General Service List of English Words*, which became a standard reference in developing teaching materials.

Structures and vocabulary thus selected are initially presented orally in meaningful situations and then practised orally in similar situations.

The S-O-S approach is based on the following principles:

- *Language is primarily speech.* Selected structures and vocabulary are presented and practised orally. As in the case of the mother tongue, the spoken form is picked up by learners before reading and writing. The order advocated for the learning of the language skills is listening (L) → speaking (S) → reading (R) → writing (W).
- *A language is a set of habits.* Practice of language items is considered necessary because a language is a set of habits, and language learning is said to be habit formation. The exponents of the S-O-S approach were strongly influenced by the operant conditioning theories of B.F. Skinner, according to which habits are established when reward or reinforcement follow. Reinforcement is a vital element in the learning process, because it increases the likelihood that the behaviour will occur again and ultimately become a habit.

The behavioural psychology of Skinner which is also known as the 'stimulus-response theory' of learning was found to be relevant in the S-O-S approach, which, as a result, led to pattern-drilling, mimicry, memorisation, etc. According to Rivers (1968), the learners 'learn to manipulate structures to a point of automatic response to a language stimulus'. Thus, 'Palmer points out that there are three processes in learning a language—receiving the knowledge or materials, fixing it in the memory by repetition, and using it in actual practice until it becomes a personal skill' (Frisby 1957).

In the situational approach, explanations are discouraged and the learner is expected to apply the language learnt in the classroom to situations outside the classroom. By using situations, the use of the mother tongue can be avoided. If the language item is given in meaningful situations, the learners can deduce the meaning and context from the situation in which it is used. The approach finds support in the writings of F.L. Billows and G.A. Pittman.

> If we give the meaning of a new word either by translation into the mother tongue or by an equivalent in the same language as soon as we introduce it, we weaken the impression which the word makes on the mind.
>
> Billows 1961

> … the situation will be controlled carefully to teach the new language material … in such a way that there can be no doubt in the learner's mind the meaning of what he hears.
>
> Pittman 1967

Pittman suggests that 'almost all the vocabulary and structures taught in the first four or five years of learning English and even later can be placed in situations in which the meaning is quite clear' (ibid.). Situations are denoted by the use of concrete objects, pictures and realia, which, together with actions and gestures, can be used to demonstrate the meaning of new language items.

The characteristics of the S-O-S approach can be summarised as follows.

- Speech is the basis of language teaching—new language items and vocabulary items are presented orally before they are presented in the written form.
- The language items which are commonly used by native speakers in their day-to-day language are selected for teaching.
- The items are also graded according to their usefulness, frequency and teachability.
- The language items thus selected and graded are presented and practised in meaningful situations.
- Vocabulary items are selected with reference to the General Service List.
- Reading and writing are based on items which have already been introduced and practised orally.

THINK IT OVER

1. When we learn our mother tongue, is our language input graded?
2. Is the LSRW order followed strictly in all language situations?

Syllabus

Basic to the teaching of English as a second language is a structural syllabus and a word list. A structural syllabus is a list of the basic structures and sentence patterns of English according to their order of presentation. The syllabus is generally prepared by a team of language experts and methodologists. In southern India, the syllabus usually consisted of about 250 structures or language items and 2500 to 3000 vocabulary items spread over a period of seven years in the case of Tamil Nadu and five years in the other states.

Look at a sample of the typical structural syllabus.

First year of English

Language items

1. This is a …
2. It's red/green/yellow, etc.
3. These are books/boys/girls.
4. This is Ram/Padma.
5. He's a boy./She's a girl./It's a bag.
6. present continuous tense
7. prepositions

Second year of English

Language items

1. We're boys/girls/men.
   They're boys/girls/men.
   You're boys/girls/men.
2. What're these/those?
   Are they bags/balls?
3. There's a …
4. Is there a …?
5. How many … are there?

Third year of English

Language items

1. simple past tense—affirmative
   (common irregular verbs—singular, plural, all persons)
2. simple past tense—interrogative
3. simple past tense—negative
4. adverbs + adverbial phrases of time
5. 'first', 'last', 'next' …

Texts

The textbooks are based on the structural syllabus, and they are specially prepared to allow use of the S-O-S approach. They consist of lessons which introduce the language items and vocabulary included in the syllabus of English for the class or year concerned. Experts who are specially appointed to write these lessons choose interesting contexts well within the conceptual level of the class to present the language items and the vocabulary. They take care to see that the items to be introduced are meaningfully spread over the whole lesson and not huddled together in one of the paragraphs.

The lessons are in the form of descriptions, narrations, dialogues, letters and plays. They are generally divided into three parts. The first part deals with the preparatory materials for the teacher. It lists out the new language items and the vocabulary at the top, and suggests situations for introducing them. The second part consists of the reading passage. The third part provides a number of useful exercises for the consolidation of the new language items and vocabulary that have been introduced in the lesson.

Think it over

1. What sort of lessons (reading passages) would a textbook writer produce? Would they be natural?
2. How far would these texts and the syllabus prepare learners to tackle communication?

Techniques used in the S-O-S approach

Situations

In the S-O-S approach, structures are always presented in meaningful situations. First, the language item is presented and practised orally and this is followed by practice in reading and writing.

In the classroom

All that is available in the classroom, for example the furniture, blackboard, pictures, calendar, windows and doors, can be made use of for the presentation and the practice of new language items and vocabulary.

Outside the classroom

Things outside which can be seen from the classroom, for example, trees and flowers, can also be used for teaching.

Pictures, picture cut-outs, drawings, objects and models

Visual aids provide very effective situations in teaching. Teachers can draw stick figures on the blackboard and bring small objects which are easily available to the classroom. One of the most useful things which all teachers can afford to do is to have a good collection of pictures from old magazines, newspapers, etc.[3]

Verbal situations

Vocabulary items which cannot be taught using any of the techniques listed above will have to be explained in either the mother tongue or the target language. Words which are abstract in nature fall into this category. For instance, a word such as 'honest' or 'honesty' needs explaining.

DRILLS

The use of drills is a central technique of the S-O-S approach. Drills can be of three types: chorus, group and individual. In chorus drills, the whole class takes part in repeating the pattern or vocabulary item. For group drilling, the class is divided into groups and the patterns are practised by groups, one after another. Later, individual students are asked to drill the pattern.

Substitution table

A substitution table is a very effective teaching device which can be used to give learners mastery over English constructions. It was invented and developed by H.E. Palmer. The name derives from the fact that different words in different columns of the table can be substituted, thereby producing a large number of examples of that construction.

Look at the example on the next page. It presents the simplest pattern, expressing possession. You can get 256 sentences from this table.

[3] See Chapter 7, 'Teaching Aids', pp. 177–181.

1	2	3	4
		my	house.
		your	bottle of ink.
		our	garden.
This	is	their	goat.
That	is not	Mary's	cow.
		the doctor's	bedroom.
		his	motor car.
		her	train.

In the words of French (1960), 'The value of a substitution table lies in its use as a habit maker. Through substitution tables the learner becomes habituated to the use of correct forms and only the correct form. Habit can come only by practice, drill and memory; there is no other way.'

A substitution table can also be used as a testing table in which only certain items can be combined to frame correct and meaningful sentences. Learners will have to make a correct choice of words from the columns of the table to construct meaningful sentences.

Call-word technique–substitution

In this drill, the teacher writes a pattern on the blackboard. Learners are asked to read it a few times and once they have mastered the pattern, the teacher calls out words to be substituted in the right places in the sentence. For example:

(On the blackboard: 'The book is on the table.')

Teacher floor
Learner The book is on the floor.
Teacher bench
Learner The book is on the bench.

Similarly, the teacher asks the learners to change the other words in the sentence with the substitutes she/he provides.

Incremental drills

In this drill learners are asked to add a word/words to a sentence given by the teacher. The teacher supplies the word/words to be added. For example:

Teacher	I saw him.
Learner	I saw him.
Teacher	yesterday
Learner	I saw him yesterday.
Teacher	at ten
Learner	I saw him yesterday at ten.
Teacher	in the morning
Learner	I saw him yesterday at ten in the morning.

Backward chaining technique

This technique is useful when some learners are not able to repeat a long sentence. In this drill, words or phrases from the end of a sentence are taken and repeated. The movement is from the end to the beginning. For example:

Teacher	in the morning
Learner	in the morning
Teacher	at ten
Learner	at ten in the morning
Teacher	yesterday
Learner	yesterday at ten in the morning.
Teacher	saw him
Learner	saw him yesterday at ten in the morning.
Teacher	I
Learner	I saw him yesterday at ten in the morning.

Completion[4]

In this technique learners are given a part of a sentence or one clause, and they have to complete the sentence by adding a meaningful part or clause.

He worked so hard .... (first class).

If you drive fast .... (accident).

Unless you know the skill .... (well).

If he had known my address .... (not miss).

---

[4] See Chapter 6, 'Techniques of Teaching English', p. 140.

Transformation

This is a well-known technique where learners are required to change a statement into a question, an affirmative statement into a negative statement, an active sentence into a passive sentence.

Combining sentences or parts of a sentence

In this technique, two sentences are given and learners are asked to combine them. For example:

One must be punctual. This is important.

It is important to be punctual.

He is very rich. He can buy a palace.

He is so rich that he can buy a palace.

Inversion to avoid repetition

He works hard. I work hard too.

He works hard; so do I.

He doesn't have a car. I don't have a car either.

He doesn't have a car; nor do I.

Language laboratory

A language laboratory is a very useful device, particularly in the context of the S-O-S approach. In fact, the basis for its use is the stimulus-response-confirmation theory.[5]

THINK IT OVER

1. If these techniques are used, what sort of 'fluency' will the learners develop?
2. Is there any technique listed which allows a learner to express his/her ideas and thoughts?

Classroom procedure

Here is an example of how a structure is introduced and practised in the classroom, using the structural approach. The structure chosen for the purpose is the first conditional clause. (*If you work hard*, you will get a first class in the examination; *If you take the medicine*, you will get better, etc.)

[5] See Chapter 7, 'Teaching Aids', p. 184.

Teacher	Good morning, everyone.
Learners	Good morning, sir.
Teacher	How are you?
Learners	We're fine, thank you.
Teacher	I have brought your test papers. I am sorry to tell you that you haven't done well. No one has got more than 50 marks.
Learners	We're sorry, sir.
Teacher	That's all right. Look, if you work hard, you will do better next time. If you do better, all your teachers will be happy. If you do better, your parents will be happy.
Learners	We promise, sir, we will work hard.
Teacher	That's all right. Now took at this! What is this?
Learners	It's a lottery ticket.
Teacher	Yes, that's right. I bought it this morning. The draw is next month.
	If I win the first prize, I will get twenty lakh rupees.
	If I get twenty lakh rupees, I will build a house.
	If I have my own house, I can live comfortably.
	If the house is my own, I need not pay any rent.

The teacher repeats the last four sentences, and asks the learners to listen to him with attention. He then writes the four sentences on the blackboard.

> If I win the first prize, I will get twenty lakh rupees.
> If I get twenty lakh rupees, I will build a house.
> If I have my own house, I can live comfortably.
> If the house is my own, I need not pay any rent.

After writing the sentences on the blackboard, the teacher says to the learners:

Teacher	How much money will I get if I win the first prize?
Learners	Twenty lakhs.
Teacher	Yes. *(Repeats the whole sentence and asks the pupils to give complete sentences for the sake of practice.)*
Learners	If you win the first prize, you will get twenty lakhs.

The teacher asks the above question to:

- the class as a whole
- groups A, B, C, D
- individual learners

The learner gets practice in listening, speaking, reading and writing the structure or sentence pattern. First, the teacher reads the sentences on the blackboard and asks the class to read them after him/her. This is followed by the learners reading the sentences aloud individually from the blackboard. Next, the learners read the sentences on the blackboard silently. (While they are doing this, the teacher goes around the class and asks the weak learners to say/read the sentences to him/her.) Finally, the teacher gives writing practice to the class. He/she sets the following exercise on the structure taught. The learner has to combine the right parts from columns A and B.

A	B
a If you work hard	a your teacher will punish you.
b If you don't do your homework	b they will get a good crop.
c If I have ten thousand rupees	c you must see a doctor.
d If you have a fever	d you will get a first class.
e If the farmers use good fertilisers	e I can buy a TV set.

THINK IT OVER

1. What would a teacher's attitude be towards learner errors in such a class?
2. Is there any provision made for the learner's pace of learning (either slow or quick learners)?

CHAPTER SUMMARY

- The S-O-S approach came into being as an alternative to the direct method. It is an outcome of the experiments carried out in US army camps during World War II.
- Prominent names associated with this approach are Charles Fries, Harold Palmer and A.S. Hornby.

- The S-O-S approach is the systematic presentation and practice of carefully selected and graded grammatical structures of English in effective and meaningful situations. The approach is based on the assumption that language learning is a matter of habit formation, which involves a lot of repetition and conscious drilling of the language items.
- In this approach, language items are first taught orally. Reading and writing follow the oral work. Language is primarily speech, and therefore the spoken form is given priority over reading and writing.
- Language items are graded according to their frequency, usefulness and teachability. Learners in South Indian schools are expected to learn the use of more than 250 items before they take their school-leaving examination.

DID YOU UNDERSTAND?

1. What is the S-O-S approach? Answer in a paragraph.
2. What method of teaching does the teacher adopt in the S-O-S approach?
3. What is the role of the learner? What is the role of the teacher?
4. What, in your opinion, is the most important technique of the S-O-S approach? Why is this considered to be most important?
5. In what order are the skills taught in the S-O-S approach? Why?
6. Write a brief note on how the S-O-S approach developed in the USA and in India.

APPLICATION

Read the following passage and do the given tasks.

> It is remarkable how tough the cockroach is. He is far tougher than the dinosaur. He is not afraid of being stepped on. He is in no danger of being killed. Step on him, and his body saves him; the moment the pressure is removed, he runs away. It is easy for him to get through even the smallest cracks.

TASK 1

a. Select a structure to teach. Use suitable situations for introduction and practice.

b. Prepare a substitution table for practising the structure chosen.

c. Set another exercise for the learners to work out.

TASK 2

Write a 100–150 word paragraph for an S-O-S reader in which the structure 'so ... that' occurs at least five times.

FURTHER READING

The structural syllabus at work in India

The Seminar on the Teaching of English in High Schools, organised at Srinagar by the Central Institute of English, Hyderabad, provided an unusual opportunity for English-teaching specialists and educational administrators from all over India to compare notes and take stock of the working of structural syllabuses in Indian secondary schools during the last decade. The structural approach has become much more popular all over the country since its introduction in Madras, and it is felt that the time for an impartial assessment of its effectiveness has come. It is worth noting that, education being a state subject, the Department of Education in each of the fourteen states of the country deemed it necessary to make addition to the structural syllabus originally prepared under the influence of the University of London's Institute of Education. In some states it was mutilated beyond recognition, and a hotch-potch syllabus was produced in an attempt to reconcile the divergent claims of old and new schemes.

The Srinagar seminar, which lasted for a fortnight, profited greatly from the accumulated experience of the participants and the able guidance it received from its director, Dr V.K. Gokak, and his colleagues, Mr J.G. Bruton and Mr H.V. George. It discussed thoroughly all aspects of English teaching, and made recommendations which will have a vital bearing on the techniques, procedures and content of English teaching throughout India. It was generally agreed that the English syllabuses, textbooks, and evaluation procedures were responsible for the ineffective teaching and learning of English in high schools. The role of examinations in determining teaching methods was also recognised, and the need for the proper training of teachers was stressed.

Structural syllabuses have met with a favourable reception at the hands of English teachers all over India. They have already passed the experimental stage and the results achieved so far have convinced even the bitterest critics of the effectiveness of the structural approach in the teaching of English as a foreign language. How to make it yield maximum results in terms of the learner's achievement, even in rural and backward schools, is the crux of the whole problem, and thanks to the pioneering work done by the British Council and the Central Institute of English, sincere efforts are being everywhere made to tackle this problem realistically at seminars and workshops sponsored by the Department of Extension Services and other government and semi-government agencies.

Experience in India has revealed that, in the hands of a teacher appropriately trained, a structural syllabus can be an effective tool for teaching English. Implying an activity method, it demands initiative, resourcefulness, and imagination on the part of the teacher. It keeps the young learner keen and active. It appeals to his innate interests and helps him learn English as a skill subject through an oral-aural approach. He is no longer the passive recipient of doses of language, but an active participant in the co-operative enterprise of language-learning. Experienced and undogmatic teachers have discovered that a structural approach gives the best results and that pupils can be led a surprisingly long way into the heart of a language without ever opening a book or taking a single note. It is indeed a delightful sight to see a class buzzing with activity like a beehive as it gainfully learns by doing and speaking.

Notwithstanding all the advantages the structural approach has over other methods, including those dependent on the latest mechanical aids, we have discovered as a result of our experience in the classroom, our observation of the approach at work in the rural and urban schools of India, and by exchange of views at 'workshops' and seminars, that it is open to improvement and needs to be modified in certain respects. The following points deserve careful consideration. They will go a long way towards plugging the holes noticed in different states.

Pronunciation

The structural syllabus as followed in India during recent years has benefited greatly from work done at the University of London Institute of Education. There is, however, no provision for the teaching of English pronunciation. This is a serious defect in such a syllabus. A good pronunciation should be thoroughly inculcated right from the start. It is legitimate to expect that the teacher should pronounce well and ensure that the pupil imitates him. The modem emphasis on grading and selection, as well as on the significance of phonemes, should normally lead the teacher to concentrate primarily on the sounds that matter and on those which are most difficult for the pupils to pronounce. A comparative study of the sound systems of the pupil's mother tongue and of English will bring out the difficulties Indian children have in producing certain English sounds such as /f/, /s/, /o/, /v/, /w/, /z/, and /ʒ/, and certain consonant clusters in initial, medial, and final positions. Stress, rhythm, and intonation must find an important place in any English course. It is true that Indian English, like American English, has come to stay, but international intelligibility has to be the exclusive criterion if it claims to be called English.

Lack of uniformity

Adapting the structural syllabus to local needs should not mean changing it beyond recognition. In the Maharashtra and Gujarat states, for instance, the structural syllabus has been in force for over six years, but tagged on to the traditional grammar. The recent findings of linguistics have been completely ignored by those who framed the syllabus, which includes graded structures and controlled vocabulary side by side with traditional grammatical forms and categories borrowed from the old Latin grammar. Study of these which is unrelated to the reading book is not at all conducive to the mastery of spoken and written English. The essential points of grammar, which constitute the basic structure of English, should be woven into the texture of the reading lessons in such a way that the pupil may arrive at his own generalisations about the behaviour of the language.

Structures are closely related to grammar, but not to traditional grammar. The structural approach to language learning does not require the student to know or learn definitions of the parts of speech or of clause and sentence. In English, word order is far more important than inflexion. Contrasts of position are far more important than inflected forms of words. The Bombay syllabus has provided for separate grammar books, which have no correlation with the readers. The whole syllabus has been distributed over four years and the textbooks based on it are very bulky, violating the essential principles of the structural approach.

It is a pity that so far nobody has produced a self-contained English course for Indian children. In many states, local enterprise is encouraged at the expense of quality. What is needed is a series of textbooks embodying the principles of the structural approach, accompanied by teachers' handbooks, flash cards, supplementary readers, wall pictures, charts, and linguaphone records, so that the teachers in rural schools also can implement the approach with success. The books and materials produced by the English Language Teaching Institute, Allahabad, are a welcome step in this direction. The Union Ministry of Education should set up a special agency, in co-operation with State governments, to coordinate the teaching of English all over the country and to produce cheap textbooks satisfying the above conditions.

Need for research

A glance at the structural syllabus commonly used in India will show that it is defective in many ways. Various items have been put together under the common label of 'structures'. This may be convenient, but is inexact. The use of the conjunction 'but' is hardly a problem of structure. It is a lexical item. A band of researchers should be called upon to work on the syllabus and tackle this and related problems. Some of the structures included the syllabus have a very low frequency of occurrence in spoken English and can safely be dropped. For example, the following structures should be meant for comprehension, and their inclusion in the syllabus for drill and active use does not serve any useful purpose:

1. I will speak to his brother, since he is not there.
2. The hall has been filling up since seven o'clock.
3. See to it that he gets the book.
4. No sooner did he reach the station than the train left.
5. Poor as he is, he is honest.
6. That he died is certain.
7. Tell me the reason why you did it.
8. I shall have been reading that book.

As a result of extensive research, it is possible to discover the content words which can be taught while introducing each structure. In a recent article, I showed how new words and structures can be introduced simultaneously during the preliminary oral work that would precede a reading lesson. It should be constantly borne in mind that the grading of structures is not enough. Vocabulary and structures should be so graded and correlated that we may have an integrated approach to the teaching of English as one indivisible subject. A comparative linguistic analysis of the pupil's mother tongue and of English from the phonological, morphological, and syntactical points of view will yield fruitful results which will be of great value to the teaching of English in India.

Re-training of teachers

The paucity of adequately trained teachers has been largely responsible for the failure of all good methods of teaching English in India. Even a trained teacher has to be re-trained in the techniques of the structural approach if he is to deliver the goods. In the ultimate analysis, one would like to see the structural approach made practicable for average and below average and even downright bad schools. Only the right type of trained teacher can carry out this seemingly impossible task.

Unfortunately, most states have made no serious effort at training and re-training teachers. Thanks to the interest taken by the Department of Extension Services, seminars and 'workshops' are held at various centres, with a view to acquainting teachers of English with the techniques and procedures of the structural approach. The problem is of such magnitude that, unless state governments appoint special task forces to give short-term intensive training to English teachers at district centres, the new scheme will be in jeopardy and the standard of English will further deteriorate. Despite the old Bombay government's directive to schools to follow the structural approach, most schools in rural and urban areas still use the old grammar-translation method on the pretext that their teachers are not trained in new methods of teaching languages. Without a planned and methodical approach to the problems of language teaching in the special conditions of India, there will be no real progress in this sphere. Even in training colleges where students offer a paper which includes two special methods, English should be equated with 'two methods' and the course should have a linguistic orientation.

Duration of study

A four-year English syllabus for secondary schools with emphasis on the structural approach has failed to work successfully. There should be a seven-year syllabus, the first year being devoted exclusively to the teaching of about forty structures through oral work. Reading and writing may be introduced incidentally but no readers should be used. A small primer and a teacher's handbook containing detailed instructions about the procedure to be followed in the classroom will be of great practical use to the teachers and pupils alike.

It is a pity that in India everything comes from above, killing headmasters' and teachers' initiative. The government should leave the question of textbooks, etc., and of the duration of study to schools. It should lay down only its general policy, and should refrain from prescribing every detail from A to Z. The modern technique of drilling new words and structures in many different real contexts, until they are learnt automatically and directly associated in the mind with the objects and situations they represent, cannot be successfully practised if we have a four-year concentrated syllabus. English should be an optional subject and should be studied by such children as are likely to profit from its study by virtue of their aptitude and interests. These children should not be prevented from studying English for a longer period, for they will need it for their higher studies in science, medicine, and technology. It is ridiculous to ban the teaching of English in the lower forms of secondary schools even as an optional subject during school hours. Academic freedom can be more easily preached than practiced!

Examination reform

A structural syllabus and the traditional system of examination, the validity and reliability of which has been seriously questioned now, go ill together. The latest techniques of evaluation and testing should replace the old worn-out system of a single examination at the end of the year. Oral and written tests constructed on the lines suggested by Dr Benjamin Bloom of Chicago University will serve a useful purpose in measuring what pupils have learned. The syllabus has a definite purpose and objective, which should be carefully screened and justified on the basis of their practicability. The next step would be to determine the specific growth or development which would be brought about in pupils and the learning experiences through which the desired growth in pupils may be realised. Once this growth or behavioural change is determined, the next step would be to construct a test that would furnish evidence of whether the desired behaviour has been attained by the pupil or not. All this could be done provided the teacher has an abiding faith in the method he is going to use in the classroom. We often hear it said that, like other fads, this latest fad will also vanish in a few years and be replaced by another method. It is true that there is no finality in methodology, but it is equally true that tested and tried-out procedures are more effective than old techniques whose futility has been proved beyond doubt. Teachers should be open-minded and ready to give a fair trial to new ideas and techniques born of considerable experimental and research work.

Patel 1962

3

Modern Approaches

THE NOTIONAL-FUNCTIONAL SYLLABUS

An overview

Just as the structural approach had its genesis in a non-school environment, the notional-functional syllabus too had its roots in a non-school context.

In the 1960s and 70s, many countries in Europe were experiencing an upswing on the economic front. The result of this was a shift of labour from one country to another, usually in search of better job opportunities. Industries and other establishments soon had a sizeable workforce who did not speak the local language, and this led to problems of communication. The traditional methods of learning a language did not give the learners the skill to communicate with a supervisor or co-worker on the shop-floor.

To solve this problem, and also pursue its wider aims, the Council of Europe and the Council of Cultural Co-operation were given the responsibility of designing courses which would fulfil the needs of language learners. The aim of Project Number Four (Modern Languages) was 'improving and intensifying language learning as factors making for European understanding, co-operation and mobility'. The concepts of 'threshold level'[1], 'needs analysis'[2], 'language functions' and 'notions' were now applied to design courses, many of which were multimedia courses.

---

[1] 'Threshold level' refers to the minimal level of language proficiency which is needed to achieve functional abilities in a foreign language.

[2] 'Needs analysis' is the process of finding out the needs for which a particular group of learners is learning a language.

The ideas incorporated in these courses, meant for adults learning a second language, soon filtered down to the school level. Courses were revised and redefined, and coursebooks using the 'notional-functional syllabus' soon became an accepted part of the English syllabus in schools.

Syllabus

Two kinds of syllabuses developed almost simultaneously—the 'functional syllabus' and the 'notional syllabus'. These overlapped, however, to such an extent in terms of ideas and outcomes that very soon the term 'notional-functional' was being used singly rather than as two separate terms.

The functional syllabus was arranged in terms of functions and the language items needed for them. The table below illustrates this syllabus clearly.

Type of discourse	Skill	Function	Exponents	
			Vocabulary	Structure
spoken	speaking listening	asking for directions	bank harbour museum	Can you tell me where X is? Where is X?

The Longman Dictionary of Applied Linguistics 1985

D.A. Wilkins was the main proponent of the notional syllabus. This syllabus begins with the meanings and concepts a learner needs in order to communicate and the language needed to express them. These concepts and meanings are known as 'notions'.

Given below are some examples of notions from Wilkins (1976).

1. Semantico-grammatical categories
    a. Time: point of time, duration, time relations, frequency and sequence
    b. Quantity
    c. Space
    d. Sentential relations: for example, cases
       John drank the milk.
       The milk was drunk by *John*.
       It was *John* who drank the milk.

2. Categories of communicative function
   a. Judgement and evaluation
   b. Suasion
   c. Argument
      i. information asserted
      ii. information sought:[3] question, request
         - interrogatives
         - declaratives and question intonation
         - question words 'when', 'where', 'what', 'who', 'what+(time)', 'how+(far)', 'how+(much)'
      iii. information denied
      iv. agreement
      v. disagreement
      vi. concession

A book based on the notional syllabus would describe its content as follows.

Unit	Key expression	Notion
1	Where do you come from?	personal details
2	I need a …	needs
3	Do you like …?	likes and dislikes
4	What's it like?	describing objects
5	Where is it?	location
6	Would you like one?	offer
7	What do you usually do?	habit
8	May I …?	permission
9	Will you …?	request
10	Let's …	suggestion

As you can see, these syllabuses start from meaning and go on to language. Besides, the situation is also taken into account; what is appropriate in one situation may be totally inappropriate in another.

[3] Information seeking is likely to be an important aspect of a learner's language use.

Think it over

1. Why do we teach English in our schools?
2. Can a needs analysis be made at the school level?

Section summary

- The notional-functional approach to language teaching had its roots in a non-school environment.
- The notional-functional syllabus is based on meaning rather than on grammar or structure.
- The functional syllabus is based on functions and the language needed to express these functions.
- The notional syllabus is based on the language needed to express certain notions/ideas.

Application

Task 1

In pairs, work out the similarities between the functional and the notional syllabuses in terms of their features.

Task 2

a. Use the function of 'asking the time' to work out a brief syllabus in the following terms.

Function	Language	Skills
	vocabulary structure	

b. Describe the methods and techniques you would use to teach this at the class 7 level.

THE COMMUNICATIVE APPROACH

An overview

The development of language learning or teaching from form-based to a meaning-based approach, the move towards an eclectic approach from a rigid method, the shift from teacher-fronted to learner-centred classes, are all subsumed under the broad term *communicative approach*.

This approach is a natural extension of the notional-functional syllabus. It had already been realised that the classical paradigm afforded an unsuitable basis for the teaching of languages for communication (Trim 1981). The notional-functional syllabus threw up ideas, worked out syllabuses, and produced textbooks, and these in turn have become the basis of the communicative approach.

The difference between the notional-functional syllabus and the communicative approach is at the level they function. The notional-functional syllabus was developed for a specific purpose, or with a specific need in mind. Learning units were arranged in terms of functions and meanings. The communicative approach is rather more broad-based. It has for its goal not just communication but communicative competence.

What is communicative competence?

It is the ability, not only to apply the grammatical rules of a language in order to form grammatically correct sentences, but also to know when and where to use these sentences—in other words, to use them appropriately.

Many syllabuses have been developed under the label 'communicative approach', and each syllabus claims that it can achieve the aim of the approach, namely, that of communicative competence. All these syllabuses share certain common features:

- They are all based on a *semantically* organised syllabus, such as the notional syllabus.
- They teach the language needed in different situations, to express and understand different *functions*.
- They emphasise *appropriacy* of language use.
- They also teach the language required to perform different *tasks* (for example, solving puzzles and getting information).

Let us now consider some communicatively organised syllabuses.

Structures and functions

Brumfit (1980a) describes this model in the following words: 'The simplest proposal is to use the grammatical system as the core of the syllabus in a ladder-like series of stages and to be prepared to relate all other essential material to this series. Thus, notional, functional and situational specifications can be conceived of as a spiral round a basically grammatical core.'

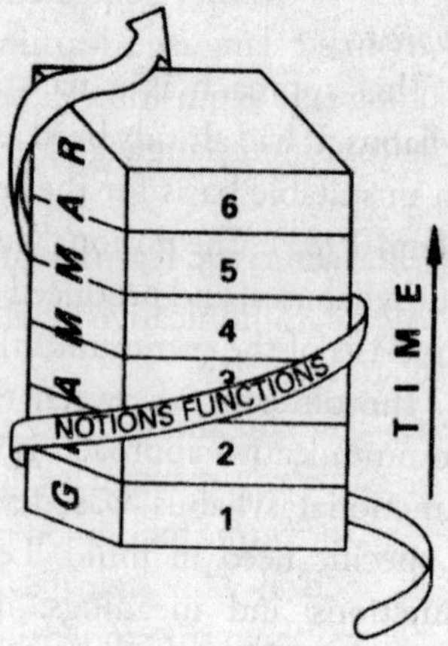

Yalden (1983) says the model represents 'a structural progression in a communicative framework'.

Variable focus

This syllabus, proposed by Allen (1980), focuses on the following aspects:

Level 1	Level 2	Level 3
Structural	Functional	Instrumental
Focus on language (formal features)	Focus on language (discourse features)	Focus on language
a. structural control	a. discourse control	a. situational/topical control
b. materials simplified structurally	b. materials simplified functionally	b. authentic language
c. mainly practice	c. mainly discourse	c. free practice

> Thus at Level 1, the main emphasis is on structural practice; functional and instrumental practice will be, relatively speaking 'out of focus'. Similarly, Level 2 emphasises functional practice, and Level 3, instrumental practice. By making use of the variable focus techniques we give recognition to the fact that there are three types of practice (structural, functional, instrumental) which interrelate, which are interdependent and which co-exist at all levels of language learning.
>
> Allen 1980

THE COMMUNICATIVE SYLLABUS

This is learner-generated and learner-centred. The focus here is to make language learning as independent of teachers as possible. Language acquisition rather than language learning takes place in this autonomous language-learning situation.

Characteristic features of the communicative approach

All communicative syllabuses are marked by the following characteristics:

- They all aim to make the learner attain *communicative competence*, that is, use language accurately and appropriately.
- The prime focus is on the *learner*. The teacher is just a facilitator—a person who 'manages' the environment and the materials which will help the students become autonomous learners.
- Communicative syllabuses rely on *authentic materials*.[4]
- The tasks set are *purposeful* and *meaningful*. This, in turn, means that a communicative task can be judged immediately for its 'success' by the learner herself/himself.
- Communicative syllabuses emphasise the *functions* of language rather than the rules.
- Communicative tasks aim to make learners *fluent* (especially during the early stages) as well as *accurate* in their use of the target language.

Techniques used in the communicative approach

In communicative language teaching, information-gap tasks are used. An information gap occurs in a situation where one person knows something which other people do not. Information-gap tasks are introduced in the classroom using the following techniques.

LANGUAGE GAMES

According to Morrow (1981), language games are communicative when they are characterised by three features: *information gap*, *choice* and *feedback*.[5]

---

[4] 'Authentic materials' here means materials which have not been produced specifically for teaching the language, as in the structural-oral-situational approach.

[5] See Chapter 6, 'Techniques of Teaching English', pp. 162–166.

Mind-engaging tasks

Communicative activities are based on the implicit recognition that a learner learns best when his/her mind is on tasks to be done *in* the language rather than *on* language itself. Thus many problem-solving activities are a part of the communicative approach.

Role play

Since the ability to manipulate language in a social context is an important aspect of communicative competence, most communicative materials include role play as a part of the activities.

Retrieving text order

The technique involves the use of scrambled sentences and scrambled picture techniques. By doing these activities, learners become aware of discourse features which are distinct from grammatical features. They become familiar with the use of cohesive devices ('and', 'or', 'nevertheless', etc.), anaphoric pronouns (the boy → he; the dog → it), and semantic clues (use of lexical items, topic, etc.) through these activities.

Group work/pair work

Group work and pair work form an important part of any communicative activity, since peer interaction is an effective means of acquiring some language features which are not available in a formal teacher-fronted class.

The language teacher

The large variety of communicative syllabuses can make a language teacher feel confused and bewildered. But what new insights has the communicative approach thrown up and what is their relevance to a class teacher? Maley (1984) has summed up the points succinctly in an article. They are as follows:

- Change of teacher and learner roles: The teacher is no longer regarded as sole arbiter and controller of what goes on in the language classroom. The *independent status* of the learner is fully accepted (if not always applied) by most theorists and practitioners.

- The importance of group supportiveness: There are now few approaches that do not harness the *group dynamic*. The group is recognised to be more than its separate components. It also offers a security system for learning.
- The importance of a relaxed atmosphere: We learn better when we are *relaxed*, and so learners should not be made to feel inadequate or threatened.
- The realisation of the hidden capacity of the human brain: Until fairly recently, we were content to believe that learning is an arduous and slow process. Contemporary research has shown that much of one's brain capacity is left unused in normal circumstances and therefore they stress the importance of *peripheral* and *subconscious learning*.
- Highlighting the role of play (in learning): Indeed, the value of the *ludic function* of language has been rediscovered and reapplied. Learning is no longer considered to be a solemn and serious activity.
- Change in the attitude towards error and error correction of learners: *Errors* are no longer regarded as sinful but are recognised as a necessary and systematic part of the learning process. The resources for correction (and self-correction) have been greatly expanded too.
- The importance of building inner criteria: Fuller realisation has come about that it is the *learners* who are *responsible* for their own learning, and the teacher's job is to help them find their own way to do it best.
- Creative silence is no longer looked upon as a waste of time: A *period of incubation* between input and output is now considered necessary as it is recognised that learners need time to work over the input internally.

THINK IT OVER

1. Does the communicative approach share any common features with the more traditional methods and approaches to teaching English?

2. Think of the drills which form an important technique in the structural-oral-situational approach. Can you think of ways of making a drill communicative?

The lesson plan given below demonstrates the use of the communicative approach in class.

Stage 1:	discussion of learner plans for the weekend (concept of planning activities and diaries)
Stage 2:	simulated input; two sets of diary entries given to learners (concept checked; practise 'making suggestions'; etc.)
Stage 3:	role play using the input
Stage 4:	information-gap exercise using two sets of information sheets (negotiating: using a wide range of language)

Input material for Stage 2

Monday			
	MORNING	AFTERNOON	EVENING
RADHA	dance class	free	dinner at club
RAMA	free	typing class	chess with Madhu
Tuesday			
	MORNING	AFTERNOON	EVENING
RADHA	hairdresser	complete school assignment	free
RAMA	free	school project practice	drama
Wednesday			
	MORNING	AFTERNOON	EVENING
RADHA	free	yoga	free
RAMA	free	cinema with friends	free

Input material for Stage 4 (Sheet 1 to go to one student, and Sheet 2 to be given to the other student in each pair)

SHEET 1

You are Ashok, studying in class 10. Your friend Sita, who lives in Mumbai, has come to Chennai on vacation. You would like to meet her and go out. Given below is your diary for the week ahead with blank spaces to indicate times when you are free. You like playing badminton and chess and listening to music. You like Chinese food and dislike North Indian food. Do not show the sheet to your partner.

	MORNING	AFTERNOON	EVENING
MONDAY	yoga		badminton
TUESDAY		library	
WEDNESDAY		tuition	Mani aunty coming for dinner
THURSDAY	yoga		
FRIDAY	yoga	tuition	Going away to Ooty

SHEET 2

You are Sita, and you are in Chennai for the summer vacation. You would like to meet your friend Ashok. Look at your diary to see when you will be free in the week ahead. You like listening to music, watching movies and reading. You love North Indian food, but you don't mind Chinese food.

	MORNING	AFTERNOON	EVENING
MONDAY		meeting Lakshmi mami	
TUESDAY	shopping with amma		dinner with appa's friends
WEDNESDAY	visiting the harbour		
THURSDAY	yoga		
FRIDAY			concert at the Music Academy

In pairs, fix up a day for meeting your friend. Discuss the time, place and what you want to do.

This should lead to the use of the language of suggestion, rejection, acceptance, confirmation, etc.

Section summary

- The communicative approach is based on a semantic syllabus like the notional-functional syllabus.
- There is no *one* communicative syllabus, only a communicative approach.
- All communicative syllabuses have some features in common.
- The communicative approach makes use of some techniques, such as the information-gap technique.
- The communicative approach has implications for the classroom teacher in terms of his/her way of teaching and attitudes.
- Teaching based on the communicative approach is eclectic.

Did you understand?

1. Trace the history of the notional-functional syllabus in not more than sixty words.
2. What is the main feature of the functional syllabus? Describe with an example.
3. List some of the notions you find in the notional syllabus. What are the language exponents for these notions?
4. In what way is the communicative approach different from the notional-functional syllabuses?
5. Explain, with examples, two communicative syllabuses.
6. Consider the quotation below in terms of the communicative approach and answer the questions that follow.

> By making it possible for the students to use language in real situations, by creating a high level of interest in the language, by diversifying the input, by activating their thinking and feeling through English, we can initiate a self-teaching or autonomous learning process. When this process has got going, our students should be able to tackle general and specific problems without any great difficulty.
>
> Bagchi 1985

a. How many of the language-learning features listed above are incorporated in the communicative approach?
b. What implications does the above quotation have for a classroom teacher?
c. What 'problems' do you think a learner is likely to encounter?
d. Do you agree with what the author says? Justify. (You can agree, disagree or partially agree.)

APPLICATION

TASK 1

Given below are some teaching aims. Choose one from each list and say how you will develop them into lessons based on the communicative approach.

List A

a. to develop listening skills at class 8 level
b. to use role play in asking for information
c. to identify lexical items related to clothing

List B

a. to teach and practise 'must' and 'mustn't' in context
b. to understand the item 'too' to mean 'more than enough'
c. to use 'used to' to express a discontinued past state

TASK 2

Given below are a few sources of authentic materials.

- a news broadcast
- an instruction leaflet (with a piece of equipment, such as a refrigerator or a washing machine)
- a recipe
- a puzzle which uses language (for example: 'Two mothers and two daughters were given three apples. Each ate an apple. How?')
- a railway timetable, a school timetable, a television programme, a weather report, etc.

a. Choose one of the above and get authentic material of its kind. Build a communicative lesson around it and explain it in just one page.
b. Write a half-page lesson plan for a forty-minute class. Remember to mention the level and the specific skills practised/used at each stage.

4

Humanistic Approaches

In this chapter we will be dealing with an area of methodology that is the latest and most thought-provoking. It has for its base not linguistic theories or pedagogic facts but something more basic—*the human being*. The methodologies being discussed under the humanistic approaches were almost all developed by people outside the language-teaching profession. They evolved because the persons were concerned about language learners. The 'caring and sharing' attitudes of these persons have shaped these methodologies.

Charles A. Curran was a Roman Catholic priest and professor of clinical psychology. His counselling sessions gave him unique insights into the workings of the minds of individuals. He understood that a language teacher could easily damage the self-image of learners (especially adult learners) from his/her position of absolute linguistic power. His approach extended the role of learners significantly. An adult learner's active participation in the learning act would ensure that his/her dignity was not damaged. The teacher was expected to be warm, supportive and give the learners non-critical understanding, especially in the initial stages.

Caleb Gattegno was a talented and creative teacher of mathematics who wanted to make learning as stress-free as possible. According to him, a fully human person was one who was a caring and constructive member of society, and education enabled a person to evolve into such a being. Therefore, the choice of the right teaching method was an important factor in the development of people. Gattegno also believed in nurturing the qualities of independence, autonomy and responsibility through the learning process, as reflected in his work *Teaching Foreign Languages in Schools: The Silent Way* (1963).

Georgi Lozanov was a psychiatrist whose participation in a surgical operation showed the power of suggestion. He assisted in an operation as an anaesthetist—only, he did not use anaesthesia, but suggestions. The operation was performed successfully and the patient was not aware of any pain. Lozanov believed that the total potential of the human brain had not been tapped, and an atmosphere free from negative suggestions would make learning joyful and easy.

James Asher was a clinical psychologist who felt that learners, particularly children, must be liberated from having to sit still so unnaturally most of the time in a classroom. A little fun in class, Asher believed, went a long way in learning.

The humanistic approaches are very interesting and exciting because they have taken language learning out of the narrow confines of linguistics and pedagogy and related them to the human being.

An overview

The humanistic approach to language teaching/learning has evolved through investigations into the nature of individuals and the philosophical conclusions drawn from these investigations. As in other approaches, the humanistic approach has drawn on pedagogic and psychological insights into the nature of learning itself.

Stevick (1990) specifies three things which a humanistic course is *not*, namely:

a. It is not a course which is taught because of some tradition or because it is a syllabus designed by an impersonal authority.
b. It is not a course in which a teacher remains 'in charge'.
c. It is not a course in which getting a good grade is the aim.

The humanistic approach tends to see language learning as a process which engages the whole person and not just the intellect. It takes into account the emotional and spiritual needs of an individual too. To state briefly the philosophy behind the approach, the ideal world should consist of 'autonomous, creative and emotionally secure people' (Brumfit 1982), and education should and can assist in the creation of such a world.

It would be useful at this juncture to quote Stevick's classification of what he considers the most important characteristics of humanism.

Feelings, including both personal emotions and aesthetic appreciation. This aspect of humanism tends to reject whatever makes people feel bad, or whatever destroys or forbids aesthetic enjoyment.

Social relations. This side of humanism encourages friendship and cooperation, and opposes whatever tends to reduce them.

Responsibility. This aspect accepts the need for public scrutiny, criticism, and correction, and disapproves of whoever or whatever denies their importance.

Intellect, including knowledge, reason, and understanding. This aspect fights against whatever interferes with the free exercise of the mind, and is suspicious of anything that cannot be tested intellectually.

Self-actualisation, the quest for full realisation of one's own deepest true qualities. This aspect believes that since conformity leads to enslavement, the pursuit of uniqueness brings about liberation.

Stevick 1990

THINK IT OVER

1. How many of the above four factors were taken into account when you did your schooling? Think back.
2. Discuss your school system in small groups or pairs. Share your experience with the whole group.

What is the humanistic approach?

Stevick's test considers humanism in very general terms. With specific regard to ELT, the *Longman Dictionary of Applied Linguistics* (1985) defines the humanistic approach as follows:

(in language teaching) a term sometimes used for what underlies methods in which the following principles are considered important:

a. the development of human values
b. growth in self-awareness and in the understanding of others
c. sensitivity to human feelings and emotions
d. active student involvement in learning and in the way learning takes place (for the last reason such methods are also said to be student-centred)

You will notice that (b), (c) and (d) focus mainly on classroom procedure, while (a) incorporates classroom procedure with materials used.

Two methods are generally considered to reflect the philosophy of the humanistic approach in the fullest measure. They are:

- The silent way
- Community language learning

Two other methods which consciously incorporate some of the tenets of the humanistic approach are:

- Suggestopaedia
- Total physical response

THE SILENT WAY

'The silent way' was evolved by Caleb Gattegno, a teacher of mathematics. In the 1960s, he proposed this method, which was based on the tenet 'teaching must be subordinate to learning'. In the silent way, the teacher is almost silent, and the learners do all the talking.

In the classroom

Equipment/aids

The two important aids that teachers of the silent way use are the *fidel chart* and *Cuisenaire rods*.[1] The fidel chart consists of blocks of different colours on a black background. Each block of colour represents a different sound in the target language. Cuisenaire rods are coloured wooden rods of different lengths, each of which stands for different words or sounds. They are used to build up words and sentences.

The method

1. The fidel chart is put up in the class. The sounds are divided into vowel sounds and consonant sounds.
2. The teacher silently points to a block with a pointer. Learners remain silent. She/he does this again. Again, there is silence. The third time, the teacher points to a block and says /a/. Soon, the class is repeating sounds. The teacher does not speak.
3. This technique is used to teach long vowels, short vowels, consonant sounds, and, finally, words.

[1] The word 'fidel' means 'alphabet'. Cuisenaire rods are used in mathematics.

4. After some time, learners come up to the front of the class and point to different blocks. The class repeats the words. There is a lot of peer interaction and peer correction. The teacher speaks only when absolutely necessary.
5. The Cuisenaire rods represent words. The teacher points to the fidel chart and taps out the word each rod represents. For example:
   the book (pink small rod)   *the table* (green big rod)
   on (black small rod)   *is* (white rod)
6. The teacher then shows the class one rod at a time and the class repeats the sentence 'The book is on the table'.
7. Further sentences are built up in this way.
8. The teacher uses a lot of gestures during the lesson. For example, if learners say /fud/ instead of /fu:d/, she/he will put her/his palms together and spread them apart to indicate a longer vowel sound.
9. Learners are usually asked to write out the sentences they have learnt.
10. For advanced learners, picture charts for vocabulary, books with an American cultural setting, and an introduction to literature are used.

THINK IT OVER

1. Answer the following with regard to the method outlined above.
   a. At what level do you think these classes are held?
   b. Can you say how old these learners are, where the classes are taking place, and how many learners there are in the class?
   c. What conclusion can you draw?
2. Would the silent way materials be of use in your class?
3. Should a teacher remain largely silent in class?
4. How can you evaluate the learners?
5. Could this method be used in regular school work?

Summary of pedagogic principles

- Teachers build on what learners already know. They follow the 'known to unknown' principle.
- Language is learnt through the basic building blocks of sounds, as sound is a common characteristic of all languages.

- The teacher's silence encourages peer interaction and group cooperation.
- Language learning is done best in a non-threatening atmosphere. The teacher is a silent 'engineer' in the class, and so the learners do not feel threatened.
- Learner errors are dealt through self-monitoring and peer correction. No disapproval is indicated by the teacher.

APPLICATION

Look at the profile of a class 7 group.

> Class strength: 60
>
> Number of years of learning English: 2 years
>
> Teaching item: 'can', 'can't'
>
> Class time: 45 minutes

In pairs or small groups, plan a lesson using the silent way. Your lesson plan could have the following format:

Equipment (Specify the number of charts and rods and what each will represent.)

....

....

....

Sentences (Specify the sentences that learners will use.)

....

....

....

....

Procedure (Specify each step.)

1. ....
2. ....
3. ....

COMMUNITY LANGUAGE LEARNING (CLL)

Community language learning was developed by Charles Curran, a Roman Catholic priest and a professor of clinical psychology. Curran worked with adults for many years, and he developed the *counselling–learning approach*, according to which the teacher was more a 'counsellor' than a figure of authority and a judge of right and wrong.

Curran discovered that adults often feel threatened in new learning situations: one, because they are coming into contact with something unfamiliar; and two, because they are afraid of appearing foolish. To counter this, the teacher must become a counsellor—a person who not only knows the target language, but who also understands the struggle learners face while learning something new. By being understanding, teachers can help them overcome their fears and work more positively towards learning a new language.

CLL takes place in groups, either small or large, and these groups form the community. This method lays emphasis on the learners' personal feelings while learning a foreign language.

In the classroom

Equipment/aids

A tape recorder is the most important aid used in the classroom.

The method

1. Learners sit in a circle. The teacher-counsellor remains outside the circle.
2. A tape recorder is placed in the centre.
3. A conversation is started. For beginners, it can be things like introducing oneself. For example, 'Hello! I am Priya. How do you do?'
4. Learners sometimes ask the teacher-counsellor for help.[2] The teacher gives the learners the language or vocabulary they need.
5. Learners operate the tape recorder and speak into it.
6. The tape is played back after the conversation is over. Learners listen and then comment on it.

---

[2] The request for help can be made in two ways: (a) The learner speaks in his/her mother tongue and asks for a translation, or (b) the learner speaks in the target language and might need help in expressing his/her request intelligibly.

7. The teacher-counsellor takes away the tape and prepares a transcript of the tape. Errors are marked (sometimes, a set of symbols are used) and copies are handed to each learner in the next class.
8. Learners do self-correction.
9. The teacher-counsellor does some remedial or follow-up work. Doubts are cleared.
10. A new conversation begins.

THINK IT OVER

The CLL method is meant mainly for adults. Do you think any part of the methodology can be adopted for teaching in schools?

Summary of pedagogic principles

- The most important principle the CLL is based on is the principle of *security*. A learner learns best when she/he feels secure. To achieve this:
    - The teacher-counsellor, who is the 'knower', remains outside the circle of learners.
    - The teacher-counsellor does not approve or disapprove of a learner's performance.
    - The teacher-counsellor uses the mother tongue of learners to explain or translate, as they feel more secure when they understand everything.
    - A community feeling is fostered so that trust is built up and the threat of a new learning situation is reduced.
- The other important principles are:
    - The learning *initiative must be with the learners* for effective learning. (Hence, even the tape recorder is operated by them.)
    - Language is for communication. So, much of the materials for learning is authentic—what the learners say and record. The focus gradually shifts from aspects of grammar and phonetics to actual *sharing of ideas, beliefs, opinions, wants and desires.*

APPLICATION

TASK 1

Record a part of your teacher-training class discussion. The recording can be for five to ten minutes. Play it to the group the next day. What is the reaction of the group? Do they feel happy or embarrassed about the recording? Are they amused or aggressive? Ask them to comment on:

- the spoken English
- the usage
- the ideas communicated

TASK 2

Make a recording of a part of your teaching practise class. After the lesson, try to find time to play back the recording to the learners. Note their reactions. Ask them to say what they feel about the class on tape. (Let them use the mother tongue to express themselves if necessary.)

TASK 3

Make a tapescript of the discussion in Task 1. Prepare a remedial lesson for two items: one on usage, and the other on spoken English, which you think must be corrected for effective communication.

SUGGESTOPAEDIA[3]

The suggestopaedia was a method advocated by Georgi Lozanov, a Bulgarian psychiatrist, parapsychologist, and doctor of medicine. It is based on the principle of joy and easiness. Much of the methodology is based on suggestology, a psychological theory which says that human beings respond to subtle clues of which they are not consciously aware. Lozanov said that we do not use our mental capacities to the full as we have within us many psychological barriers. We fear that we will not be able to do well.

Suggestopaedia is the pedagogic application of suggestion; it aims to help learners to overcome the feeling that they cannot be successful, and so removes their mental barriers to learning. It helps learners reach hidden reserves of the mind. In Bulgaria, this method is being used even in primary schools, though in the USA, Canada and Western Europe, this method is generally associated with the teaching of languages to adults. The three main principles of suggestopaedia are:

- Joy and psychorelaxation: Learners will be able to use their hidden potentials only if they feel relaxed and happy. It is in such conditions that learners will get interested and involved in meaningful activities using the new language.

[3] This is also known as 'suggestopedy'.

- Gaining access to the reserve powers of the mind
- Harmonious collaboration of the conscious and the unconscious[4]

In the classroom

EQUIPMENT/AIDS

Posters, charts, and music are used as aids. The classroom usually has comfortable chairs, in which learners can relax. The chairs are arranged in a semicircle with the learners facing the front of the room where charts and visuals are arranged. Special care is taken about the lighting.

THE METHOD

1. Learners listen to soothing music, usually something classical.
2. They are asked to close their eyes and do some relaxation exercises (like breathing exercises).
3. Learners are given new identities. They are either delegates at a conference, tourists, or people trying to get a role in a play or film.
4. Some introductory work is done by the teacher who uses mime and actions to briefly sketch out the new identities of the learners.
5. Next, a dialogue, based on functions, is distributed. The dialogue is in two columns—one column with the dialogue in the target language and the other with the translation in the mother tongue of the learner. There are also some comments in the mother tongue about the use of certain vocabulary items and grammatical structures in the dialogue.
6. The learners now listen to the dialogue being read by the teacher, usually more than once. The reading is usually accompanied by soft background music. The learners just follow the dialogue—they are not required to do anything at this stage.
7. The class ends. The learners are given the dialogue and asked to go over it.
8. In the next class, learners take roles and read portions of the dialogue, imagining themselves in the role of that character.
9. Questions are asked in the target language about the dialogue.
10. Some translation work too is done.

[4] An open, trusting and spontaneous attitude to learning must be created among adult learners. Lozanov called this 'infantilisation'.

11. The tasks learners have to do are usually connected to some pleasurable game principle; for example, the teacher throws a ball and the person who catches it does the task. Learners do peer work using the same technique.
12. After this, other activities will be done: games, role play, creative language work, etc.
13. The cycle begins again with a new dialogue.

THINK IT OVER

In the context of the Indian education system, at which level do you think the principle of joy and easiness to learning can be applied? Is it possible at all levels?

Summary of pedagogic principles

- Learning takes place best in a relaxed and happy atmosphere.
- Sufficient listening time should be given for learners to absorb the new material.
- Active participation helps in the learning of new material.
- Role play (fantasy) reduces threat and so barriers to learning can be overcome.
- The functional aspect of language should be emphasised.
- Fine arts (music, art, drama) aid suggestion and should be integrated with the teaching/learning process.
- The atmosphere, the material, methods and techniques should aim at 'infantilisation' so that learners have a childlike (open-minded) attitude to learning.

APPLICATION

TASK 1

Our classrooms do not have comfortable chairs, carpets or curtains. There are generally more than thirty-five students in a class. In such a situation, what can we do to introduce a relaxed and happy atmosphere in the classroom? Discuss in pairs/small groups, and present your solution to the class.

TASK 2

You are a class 7 English teacher. What charts or pictures concerning any five language functions would you display to encourage learning in your class? Why?

TOTAL PHYSICAL RESPONSE[5]

This method was evolved by James Asher, an experimental psychologist. It bases its principles on the way a child learns the first language. It listens to a lot of language before it attempts to speak. The child, nevertheless, follows what is said, especially commands. So in the total physical response method, listening comprehension is the basis of the course. The teacher gives commands and orders, and learners perform the action. This is said to be a meaningful way of learning a language.

In the classroom

THE METHOD

1. The teacher gives a simple command. For example: 'Stand up!' or 'Sit down!'
2. The learners respond to the command. If they do not follow the command, the teacher demonstrates.
3. Further commands are given. The teacher demonstrates new commands. The class follows. Volunteers demonstrate new commands. The class follows. The teacher writes commands on the blackboard and demonstrates.
4. The class copies down the sentences.
5. Learners are not required to speak in the initial stages.
6. Later, learners give commands and the rest of the class performs the actions.

THINK IT OVER

1. Commands (imperatives) by their very nature are autocratic and authoritative. Is it important to make commands pleasant? Why?
2. Can the whole of language be taught through commands (imperatives)?

[5] This is also known as 'the comprehension approach'.

3. Can reading and writing skills be developed through the total physical response method?

Summary of pedagogic principles

- Meaning in the target language can be conveyed best through actions.
- Learners learn best by doing things.
- Listening comprehension should precede other skills.
- Learners must be given time to absorb the new language before they are asked to speak.
- A feeling of success aids language learning. Total physical response allows learners to achieve a high degree of success.

Application

Task 1

Make a list of commands teachers usually use in the classroom. How would you use these to teach English?

Task 2

Using the total physical response method, plan how you can do action chains. Look at the action chain below on instructions for making tea, for example.

(Learners mime the actions.)
Fill the kettle.
Light the stove.
Boil the water.
Pour it into the pot with tea leaves.

At what level would you use this for teaching?

Chapter summary

- The humanistic approach developed in the 1970s. It used insights from psychology and pedagogy, and defined in broad terms what teaching should or should not be. The two important methods used under this approach are:
  - The silent way: This was evolved by Caleb Gattegno, a mathematician. This method uses fidel charts and Cuisenaire rods. The teacher is only a facilitator and speaks very little.

    - Community language learning: The method was proposed by Charles Curran, a priest, psychologist and counsellor, who wanted learning to take place in an anxiety-free atmosphere. He proposed that the teacher take an unobtrusive role and just aid the learners in learning the language. The learners form a community, and they help each other to learn the target language.

- The other two methods are:
    - Suggestopaedia (suggestopedy): This method was developed by Georgi Lozanov of Bulgaria. He, too, believed in reducing the anxiety factor in a learning situation. He believed that fear of failure and anxiety created barriers and the true potential of a human mind could not be realised. As he was a psychiatrist, he used suggestion as an anxiety-reducing and barrier-removing tool. His classes included fine arts (especially music) as an integral part of the lesson. The functional aspect of the target language is emphasised.
    - Total physical response: This was evolved by James Asher, an experimental psychologist, who believed that much of the way in which a child learnt the mother tongue could be duplicated in a foreign-language learning situation. His method consists of commands which are followed by learners. Learners do not speak until they are ready to.

Did you understand?

1. Define the humanistic approach. What are the five important characteristics of this approach?
2. What are the main principles of Gattegno's 'silent way'?
3. In what important aspect has Curran's experience as a counsellor influenced community language learning? In what way is it realised in the classroom?
4. a. What are the three main principles on which Lozanov's suggestopaedia is based?
   b. What is infantilisation? How does it affect learning?
5. What important principle of language learning does Asher base his total physical response method on? What skill is emphasised in the method?

Application

Task 1

List three pedagogic principles which are common to all the four methods described above. How are the principles different from those of earlier language-learning methods?

Task 2

List five points based on the humanistic approach for a classroom teacher. (For example: Be kind in the class. It is better than being dictatorial.)

Task 3

You have studied many teaching methods and approaches. Each of them has an element of humanism. Match each method below with the right humanistic element.

Grammar-translation	the ability of the human mind to create new behaviour on the basis of old, well-established behaviour
Audio-lingual	the ability of the human mind to reason and decipher
Communicative approach	the relationship between discourse and life, between sentence and meaning

Task 4

List five methods or techniques of the humanistic approach which you think you can use in the Indian situation. Against each, write the class you will teach and the materials you will need.

	Method/Technique	Class	Materials
1			
2			
3			
4			
5			

FURTHER READING

Humanistic approaches: An empirical view

Teaching is an art in which the relationship between human beings, between teacher and taught, is crucial to real success. This is one way of distinguishing teaching from training, for the latter can be successful simply via a series of instructions, but the former, necessarily involving basic moral and psychological issues, engages the whole persons of both teachers and learners. However, having said this, it is difficult to add a great deal that is illuminating to those who have not experienced teaching already. Learning to teach is not to pick up formulae but to act on internalised principles—to borrow terminology from religious instruction, we are concerned not with outward and visible signs, but with inward and spiritual graces. The signs are the conventions of particular times and places, but the internal motivation and sensitivity of the good teacher will transcend the limitations of particular local conventions through the process of relating to people—the class. Each teacher re-creates the principles of teaching in relation to each new class and each new student. Some teachers do it better than others, of course, but all teachers will attest to gradually getting a 'feel' for teaching as they become more experienced. We can analyse this feeling, but the analysis will not lead to experience—it must come after the event—and the event can only occur in the process of teaching. Analysis concerns itself with facts; teaching 'feel' is concerned with values, but in the public domain we only have facts available for scrutiny, for we cannot live values in print, we can only refer to them, and careful reference turns rapidly to analysis.

Brumfit 1982

5

Other Methods: Short Notes

This is a short notes chapter, where certain other methods, namely, the direct method, audio-lingual method, reading method, bilingual method and communicational language teaching, are discussed. The methods have been tried out earlier with varying degrees of success. The common aspect of these is that certain important features of the methods have been absorbed by pedagogy. For example, when questioned about the use of the mother tongue in the classroom, a teacher might say, 'I use it only to put across concepts'. This is an important feature of the bilingual method which most of us have forgotten.

The methods mentioned above are valuable to us even today for their distinctive features. While reading this section, try to see if the beliefs you have about teaching have their roots in any of these methods.

THE DIRECT METHOD

The roots of the direct method go as far back as the nineteenth century. In 1880, Francois Gouin wrote a book called *The Art of Teaching and Learning of Languages*. According to the book, a foreign language could be taught using a series of simple events. The teacher described each event in the foreign language and set reading and writing tasks on these lessons. The teacher used *complete sentences* (rather than words and phrases) in the foreign language as input. No translation was used. This method, though not popular in France, found a ready audience in Germany.

In the late nineteenth and early twentieth century, Henry Sweet (1845–1912), an English philologist, set about modifying and improving the 'direct method', as it was called by the turn of the century. The aim of the direct method was to get the learner to *think* in the target language.

Principles of the direct approach

The teaching methodology was based on the following principles:

- The process of learning is essentially one of forming associations—speech with appropriate action, and words with concepts and objects. The associations have to be direct, concrete and definite, and cross associations which conflict with each other are to be avoided.
- Repetition is essential if associations have to be formed and reinforced. The teacher should begin with a limited number of items.
- Memory depends not only on repetition, but attention and interest as well. So, if a learner is motivated and wants to learn a language, she/he will do it.
- The teaching materials, namely, texts, dictionaries and grammar, should be interrelated and coordinated to make learning effective.
- Formal teaching of grammar should be done only after learners have intuitively absorbed it from the texts. There should be no memorisation of word lists, verb inflection, etc. Grammar teaching should begin at the sentence level (and not word level) as syntax is the most important part of grammar.

Stages of learning

Sweet divided the learning of a target language into five stages.

1. *Mechanical:* Pronunciation of words and sentences are mastered thoroughly.
2. *Grammatical:* The grammatical categories in the text are identified and taught. The teaching of grammar is graded from easy to difficult.
3. *Idiomatic and lexical:* Idioms in the text and other sources are taught systematically.
4. *Literary:* Graded texts from contemporary literature are studied.
5. *Archaic:* Older literature with particular emphasis on its lexical and syntactical items is studied.

In the classroom—a simulation

A class which used a direct method textbook would have been conducted in the following way:

Step 1 During this part of the lesson, learners listen to the target language.

Teacher (touching the blackboard) The blackboard is black.
(showing a piece of chalk) This piece of chalk is white.
(holding up a book) This book is red.
(pointing to another book) That book is green.
(holding up a piece of paper) This piece of paper is yellow.
(pointing to a desk) That desk is brown.
(holding up a pencil) Is this pencil green or is it blue? It's blue.
(opening a book) This is page seven.
Is this page five or seven? It's page seven.

Step 2 In the next stage, the teacher asks the learners questions and gets them to answer in the target language. The questions are distributed among learners in the class, or they may answer in chorus.

Teacher Is this piece of chalk white or blue?
Learner It is blue.
Teacher It's blue.
Learner It's blue.
Teacher Is this piece of paper green or is it yellow?
Learner It's yellow.
Teacher (correcting the pronunciation of 'yellow') It's yellow.
Learner It's yellow.
Teacher Class, repeat 'yellow'.
Class Yellow.

Step 3 Other items are introduced later.

Teacher Look at the desk. What colour is it?
Learner It's brown.
Teacher Look at the book. What colour is it?
Learner It's green.
Teacher Is it yellow?
Learner No, it isn't.
Teacher Look at the desk. What colour is it?
Learner It's brown.
Teacher Look at the wall. What colour is it?
Learner It's white.

The exercises normally consist of questions/answers based on what is done in the class. Some blank-filling and transformation exercises too are included. A small passage for dictation is invariably included. Given below is a sample lesson from *A Direct Method English Course: Book I* (revised edition) by E.V. Gatenby (1958).

LESSON EIGHT

WRITING AND DRAWING

That boy is drawing a glass on a piece of paper. He is not writing, he is drawing. I am writing the word 'glass' on the blackboard. Now I am making the figures 6, 7, 8 and 9. I am counting the letters in the word 'glass'. There are five letters. I am counting the figures. There are four figures on the blackboard. There is one word.

Go to the blackboard.
Take a piece of chalk.
Draw three boxes on the blackboard.
Draw two tables.
Are there three boxes on the blackboard?
Yes, there are.
Are there two tables?
Yes, there are.

Write the word 'newspaper'.
Is there one word on the blackboard?
Yes, there is.

Put six books on the table.
Are there ten books on the table?
No, there aren't.
How many books are there on the table?
There are six books on the table.

Put seven matches in the box.
How many matches are there in the box?
There are seven matches in the box.

Go to the blackboard.
Take a piece of chalk.
Write the word 'teacher'.
What are you doing now?
I am writing the word 'teacher'.
How many letters are there in the word 'teacher'?
There are seven letters.

There are three books on the table.
Go to the table.
Take two books and put them on your desk.
Are there three books on the table?
No, there aren't. There is one.
How many books are there on your desk?
There are two.
Is there a picture on his desk?
No, there isn't.

Make a letter 'r'.
Is that a letter 'r' or a letter 's'? It's a letter 'r'.

Make a figure 9.
Is that a figure 9 or a figure 8? It's a figure 9.
Is it a figure 7? No, it isn't.

Take the duster and clean the board, please.
What are you doing? I am cleaning the board.
What is he (she) doing? He (she) is cleaning the board.
What am I doing? You are making the figure 8.

How many windows are there in this room?
How many walls are there? There are four walls.
Are there five walls? No, there aren't.

Go to my table and count the books.
How many are there?
Are you standing near the table or under the table?
What colour is your pencil? It's black.
Where is your notebook?
There is one book on my table.
Is there one book on my table? Yes, there is.
Is there a piece of chalk on the table? Yes, there is.
Is there a piece of paper? No, there isn't.

Exercise

A. Answer these questions.
1. How many letters are there in the word 'writing'?
2. Are there desks in this room?
3. Are there books on your desk?
4. How many are there?
5. Is there a picture on your desk?
6. What is there near the door?
7. Are there words and figures on the board?
8. Is the teacher cleaning the board?
9. What is the teacher doing now?
10. Are you reading a book or writing a book?

B. Put into the plural. (For example: He is drawing on a piece of paper. → *They are* drawing on a piece of paper.)
1. The notebook is on the table.
2. There is one notebook on the table.
3. There is a word on the board.
4. Where is the piece of paper?
5. The glass is near the ruler.

C. Make words from these letters. (For example: 'rean' → *near*)

urrle	thsu	notuc	keat
nelac	grifeu	net	rodo

Dictation

We are writing in our notebooks with our pencils or pens. Now we are writing the word 'pupil'. How many letters are there in the word 'pupil'? I am counting the letters. One, two, three, four, five. My friend is counting too. There are five letters in the word 'pupil'. The teacher is going to the board. He is taking a piece of chalk and writing words on the board. We are writing them in our notebooks. We are not making figures. Is there a figure on the board?

A direct method classroom

The excerpt below describes how a direct method class worked.

> A direct-method class provided a clear contrast with the prevailing grammar-translation classes. The course began with the learning of the foreign words and phrases for objects and actions in the classroom. When these could be used readily and appropriately, the learning moved to the common situations and settings of everyday life, the lesson often developing around specially constructed pictures of life in the country where the language was spoken. Where the meaning of words could not be made clear by concrete representation, the teacher resorted to miming, sketches, or explanations in the foreign language, but never supplied native language translations. From the beginning the students were accustomed to hearing complete, meaningful sentences which formed part of a simple discourse, often in the form of a question–answer interchange. Grammar was not taught explicitly and deductively as in the grammar-translation class but was learned largely through practice. Students were encouraged to draw their own structural generalisations from what they had been learning by an inductive process. In this way, the study of grammar was kept at a functional level, being confined to those areas which were continually being used in speech. When grammar was taught more systematically, at a later stage, it was taught in the foreign language with the use of foreign-language terminology.

> When students were introduced to reading material, they read about things they had already discussed orally, the teacher preparing the students for reading selections by a preceding oral presentation of new words and new situations. Texts were read aloud by the teacher and the students, and the students were encouraged to seek direct comprehension by inferring meanings of unknown elements from the context, rather than by seeking equivalents in a bilingual list. Where the meaning could not be discovered in this way the teacher gave explanations in the foreign language. Students were never asked to translate passages into their native language; instead, their apprehension of the meaning was tested by questioning and discussion in the foreign language. They learned to write the language first of all by transcription, then by composing summaries of what they had been reading or simple accounts of what had been discussed. The classroom was continually filled with the sound of the foreign language, and all activity was closely linked with its use in speech and writing.
>
> Rivers 1968

APPLICATION

In groups of four or five, prepare an imaginary talk by Henry Sweet, describing the direct method. Give concrete examples for each stage of your talk. The talk should be for five minutes.

THE AUDIO-LINGUAL METHOD

This method was developed mainly in America in the 1960s and 70s. The audio-lingual method tried to demonstrate the fact that a language teaching method can be based on rigorous scientific disciplines like linguistics and psychology.

The roots of the audio-lingual method can be traced back to the language teaching programmes devised in America during the Second World War. Its focus was on the learner's ability to gain the communicative skills required in everyday discourse, particularly the skills of listening and speaking in the target language.

William Moulton of Princeton University enumerated five slogans which formed the basis of the audio-lingual method.

- Language is speech, not writing.
- A language is a set of habits.
- Teach the language, not about the language.
- A language is what native speakers say, not what someone thinks they ought to say.
- Languages are different.

As you can see, these slogans are influenced by behaviourist psychology and structural linguistics.[1]

Main features of the audio-lingual method

- The audio-lingual method treated each language skill separately: listening, speaking, reading, writing.
- This method focused primarily on the skills of listening and speaking, in accordance with Moulton's first slogan 'Language is speech, not writing'.
- The skills of writing and reading were not neglected, but the focus throughout remained on listening and speaking.
- Dialogues formed the main feature of the audio-lingual syllabus, and they were the chief means of presenting language items. They also provided learners an opportunity to practise, mimic and memorise bits of language.
- Pattern drills were an essential part of this method and used as an important technique for language teaching/learning.
- The language laboratory was introduced as an important teaching aid. It gave learners an opportunity to mimic a model and memorise language patterns.
- Like the direct method, the audio-lingual method too tried to avoid the use of the mother tongue, though perhaps not so rigidly.

---

[1] Structural linguistics: This approach in linguistics sees language as a system of different units, sounds, words and sentences, within a system. The term 'structural linguistics' is used to describe the work of American linguists like Bloomfield and Fries.

Techniques of the audio-lingual method

- The skills were taught in the following order: listening → speaking → reading → writing. The first few stages concentrated on listening and speaking skills.
- Language was introduced through dialogues which contained common structures used in everyday communication as well as useful vocabulary. The dialogues were memorised line by line. Learners mimicked the teacher or a tape, listening carefully to all the features of the spoken target language. Native speaker-like pronunciation was important in presenting the model.
- Phrases and sentences of a dialogue were learnt through repetition, first by the whole class, then by smaller groups and finally by individual learners.
- To consolidate what was learnt, the dialogue was adapted and personalised by application to the learner's own situation. These drills were practised orally, first in chorus and later individually. Some generalisations (not rules) were given to advanced learners about the structures they had practised.
- Reading and writing were introduced in the next stage. The reading material was generally based on the oral lesson in order to establish a relationship between speech and writing. All reading material was introduced orally first.
- Writing, in the early stages, was confined to transcriptions of the structures and dialogues learnt earlier. Once the learner had mastered the basic structures, she/he was asked to write reports/compositions based on the oral lessons.
- Graded passages from literary texts were introduced at an advanced stage. The learner first listened to a taped version of the text and discussed questions and answers orally. This was followed by reading and writing exercises.

Comment

The audio-lingual method showed an easy way to learn languages without burdening the intellect with problem solving as in the grammar-translation method. In a way, it democratised the learning of foreign languages.

Speaking was finally recognised as being primary to language learning. The technique it used, of graded structural practice, was a practical way of doing away with translation in the classroom. Though the audio-lingual method fell out of favour due to various factors, some of its features still find a place in classroom teaching of foreign and second languages the world over.

APPLICATION

TASK 1

Read the transcript of a telephone conversation and answer the questions that follow it.

Anne Hello, Jim. It's Anne. I've got a free afternoon. Have you got time enough for lunch with me?

Jim Sorry, I haven't. Why?

Anne Well, I've got an advertisement here for a second-hand Mercedes. It's got a stereo, air-conditioning, bullet-proof glass, calf-leather upholstery ...

Jim And has it got a video?

Anne Yes, it has.

Jim I'm sure it has, Anne. But we haven't got enough money!

a. What is the main structure used in this dialogue?
b. Prepare an exercise to practise the structure you have identified in (a).

TASK 2

a. Prepare a one-page, thirty-minute lesson plan according to the audio-lingual method, using the conversation given below.

   A I'm sorry to hear that *your mother's ill.*

   B Thank you. I'm glad to say *she's better now.*

   A I'm glad to hear it.

b. How would you personalise the conversation? (Clue: Look at the italicised parts of the conversation).

THE READING METHOD

The reading method developed entirely for pragmatic reasons. Michael West, who taught in India, argued that for Indians the ability to read fluently in English was more important than speaking in English. To this end, he developed the reading method. After studying the American high school scene, Coleman (1929) decided that the only practical way to teach a language was to concentrate on reading skills.

It is interesting to note here, that whereas West's ideas continue to find a place in our language policies (English as a library language), they were thrown out quite early in America, before the World War. The criticism of the reading method below sums up the reaction in America.

> It is very doubtful whether students of short courses in high schools were ever able to read ungraded material with ease and direct comprehension at the end of the course. As soon as they encountered ungraded material they were forced back into deciphering with the aid of a dictionary, and valuable training in the reading skill was wasted. As a justification, for short language courses, the reading aim was thus spurious .... The reading method for the most part produced students who were unable to comprehend and speak the language beyond the very simplest of exchanges.
>
> Rivers 1968

The Indian reaction, in West's centenary year was, however, different.

> For ELT in India today, however, West's work appears to have three lessons which we would like to draw in three brief statements. First, that good ELT must risk allowing theory to be judged in ordinary classrooms. Secondly, that curriculum renewal is a problem in education as a whole and not just language education and it therefore has to be based on neutral studies of the educational system in all its essentials. And lastly, that the four areas West singled out for deep study and analysis, namely, Indian multilingualism, reading and its teaching, vocabulary studies and word teaching, and materials design and development ought to be focused as much today as they were by him in his day; in this centenary year of West's birth there is once again the need to address the priorities in English language teaching.
>
> Tickoo 1988

The objective of the reading method was to make learners fluent readers. Comprehension, and not reproduction, was the aim.

Syllabus and methodology

In a reading method class, the first few weeks were spent in oral work so that a strong bond between sound and print could be created to facilitate 'inner speech'. Then the reading text was introduced. Oral work of some sort continued, for the teacher or learners would often read aloud from texts in the class.

Texts

The reading texts were graded in terms of vocabulary. The texts were divided into two kinds.

- *Intensive reading texts:* The texts were taught and practised through strategies such as inferring meaning from the context, anaphora, etc., and grammatical points were discussed. Comprehension was checked mainly through questions and answers.
- *Extensive reading texts:* Here speed and overall comprehension was the aim. Learners read these texts at their own pace.[2] As in the direct method, translation was not encouraged. The learner was encouraged to infer the meaning from contextual clues.

Features of the reading method

The development of the reading method introduced some new features into the English language teaching field.

- the notion of vocabulary grading, which is even today the basis of graded readers produced by publishing companies
- the creation in a systematic way of grading readers
- the concept of extensive or 'rapid' reading in a foreign language
- the idea that techniques to teach one skill of language (reading) could be developed comprehensively; and also, that such courses could be taught

APPLICATION

Find four passages of 150 words each to teach intensive reading. Say how you will grade them. Prepare questions to test the learner's comprehension of these passages.

or

Find four passages (folk tales, anecdotes, descriptions, etc.) of 250 words each for extensive reading. Grade the passages. Prepare questions to test the learner's understanding of the gist of the passages.

[2] Based on the principles he advocated, Michael West produced a series of books, the *New Method Readers*, for use in the classroom.

THE BILINGUAL METHOD

The bilingual method proposed by C.J. Dodson tried to incorporate different aspects of the direct method and the grammar-translation method to evolve an effective second-language teaching method. Dodson (1967) believed that

> … in some emergent countries, where a major world language is being taught as a second language to young children by the direct method, … if this type of teaching were successful … the vernacular would disappear within a few generations. It is only possible to teach a second language by direct-method techniques at the expense of the first language and it is sheer hypocrisy to claim that the final aim of such teaching philosophies is bilingualism.

So, in the bilingual method, the use of the mother tongue is allowed (but it is strictly controlled and limited to concept translation).

Syllabus and methodology

The bilingual method is built around situations. All language skills are considered equally important and no skill is 'postponed' to a later time. Fluency in language skills is achieved in each situation. Mastering of skills is not seen as a long-term, painful process. The focus is, in the early stages, on oral or conversational proficiency, and this is to be achieved in each situation, whatever its range.

The steps of the methodology are as follows:

1. Imitation of basic foreign-language (FL) sentences (basic situation)
2. Interpretation of basic sentences in FL (basic situation): This step comes after the learners have become fluent in pronouncing the basic sentences in the FL. The teacher gives an oral mother tongue (MT) stimulus for evoking the FL response of the learner.
3. Substitution and extension of FL sentences (extended situation): The learner is able to speak independently about limited situations without an oral or printed stimulus.
4. Independent speaking of sentences (basic and extended situation): The learner begins to speak related sentences without a spoken stimulus either in the MT or FL.

5. Reverse interpretation (optional; basic and extended situation): Here the teacher gives a FL stimulus and the learner responds in the MT.
6. Interpretation of questions (if not undertaken in Steps 1 and/or 3): This is basically the question–answer stage, and learners are taught question forms separately so that the question patterns are consolidated before they respond to questions in the FL.
7. FL questions and answers (basic and extended situations)
8. Normal FL conversation (basic, extended and original situations): This is the final step where the learners converse independently in the FL.

The steps involved in the bilingual process are as follows:

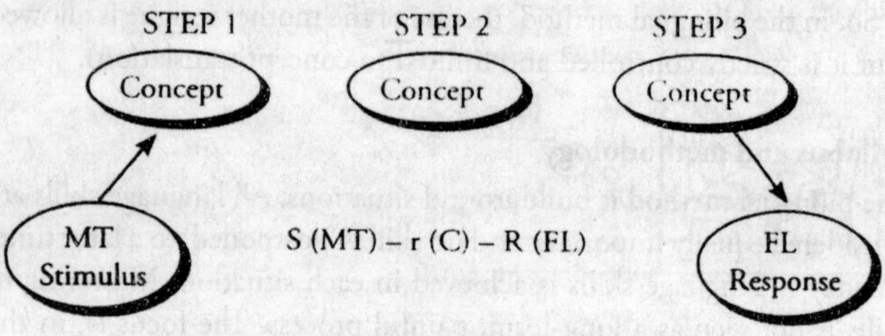

S = stimulus; r = intermediary; R = response

> In Step 1, the mother-tongue stimulus causes the concept. In Step 2, the concept becomes divorced from the original stimulus which is then blocked, whilst the concept in turn becomes the new stimulus for the foreign-language response. In other words there is no link between the MT and the FL at the time the response is made …
>
> ibid.

The aim of the bilingual method is to:

- help the learner to speak fluently and accurately in the target language.
- help the learner to write fluently and accurately in the target language.
- prepare the learner in such a manner that she/he can achieve true bilingualism.[3]

[3] A 'true bilingual' is described as a person who can jump from one language to another easily, and talk fluently about any situation in either the mother tongue or the target language with equal ease.

Texts

The texts or materials are quite short and profusely illustrated. According to Dodson each situation should be illustrated to aid the conceptualisation process in learners. As you can see, the basic skill on which this method really focuses is the speaking skill. Reading is to a large extent confined to deciphering the stimuli. Writing comes at a much later stage.

A typical example of a situation used in the bilingual method is given below.

Text

'Hello, Peter.'

'Hello, Paul.'

'Let's go to the café and have a cup of coffee.'

'All right. I am a little thirsty.'

They walk quickly to the bus stop. They do not have to wait a long time before the bus arrives. At eleven o'clock they arrive at the café.

They enter the café and sit down at a corner table. The waiter comes to the table and asks:

'What would you like, boys?'

'Two cups of coffee, please, without sugar.'

ibid.

Comment

The bilingual method adopts different methods and techniques—in fact, anything which furthers its method—of *effective* teaching. Perhaps Dodson's philosophy gives us a clue as to why this is done:

> Theories are often new interpretations of old facts and theories satisfy only those who wish to be satisfied.
>
> ibid.

Dodson admits that activities have been taken from many methods, but that these have been 'systematised into a new synthesis'. The bilingual method has greatly helped to free teachers from a feeling of guilt for using the mother tongue occasionally in the classroom. Experiments with the method have been done at the Central Institute of English and Foreign Languages (now, the English and Foreign Languages University), Hyderabad.

APPLICATION

TASK 1

Given below are some words.

honesty	desert (n)	camel	daffodil
tent	cruelty	beauty	respect

If you were using the bilingual method …

a. Which words would you translate?
b. Which words would you illustrate using aids, pictures, etc.? (Clue: Which words describe concepts?)

TASK 2

In the bilingual method, at what stage would you use a substitution table like the one below?

Who		in the room?
What	is	on the table?
Where		the boy?
Which		the pencil?

TASK 3

Given below is a brief outline of a situation.

John, William and Mary go into a milk bar. They go to the counter. Mr Jones asks them, 'What would you like this morning?' William replies, 'Three milkshakes, please.'

a. How many illustrations would the above require?
b. Would this situation be familiar to the majority of Indian learners?

COMMUNICATIONAL TEACHING

Communicational teaching refers to a five-year project of exploratory teaching of English as a second language which was

> ... planned, carried out and reviewed regularly by a group of interested teacher trainers and teachers of English as a part-time activity but with institutional support from the Regional Institute of English, Bangalore, and the British Council in Madras from 1979 to 1984 .... The stimulus for the project was a strongly felt pedagogic intuition arising from experience generally but made concrete in the course of professional debate in India. This was that the development of competence in a second language requires not systematisation of language inputs or maximisation of planned practice (features of the S-O-S approach), but rather the creation of conditions in which learners engage in an effort to cope with communication. In the context of the project, competence in a language was seen as consisting primarily of an ability to conform automatically to grammatical norms, and communication as a matter of understanding, arriving at, and conveying meaning.
>
> Prabhu 1987

The focus of the project, as Prabhu says, was not on communicative competence but rather on *grammatical competence* which was supposed to develop in the course of meaning-focused activity in the English class.

Features of communicational teaching

- There is no systematicity in terms of structures or teaching items and situations.
- Problem-solving activities or tasks form the main thrust of teaching and learning. Learners are encouraged to attain facility with the language through these activities.
- In dealing with the class, the teacher controls his/her language as an adult does while talking to a child. This is known as natural control.[4]
- In communicational teaching the learner has to engage with more than one language item that are required for problem-solving activities at the same time.

[4] In the S-O-S approach, the teacher's language is controlled by syllabus items that she/he is supposed to be teaching.

- Production of a language item (using the language item) need not necessarily follow the reception of it. With natural language acquisition there is a prolonged period of absorption. At some point, the learner begins to produce language relevant to the situation and this picks up rapidly. (In the S-O-S approach, learners are made to listen to a language item for a few minutes and then asked to say or repeat the item.) The period of absorption can be called the incubation period with reference to language learning.

Syllabus and methodology

To begin with, the main focus of the project team was on methodology. The team explored ways of focusing the attention of the learners on meaning, and not on forms of language. This gave rise to what is called the procedural syllabus. Thus the Communicational Teaching Project (CTP) syllabus contained no linguistic specifications at all but instead comprised a series of tasks in the form of problem-solving activities. The central tenet of the CTP was that language form was best learnt when the learner's attention was on meaning and not form:

> Grammar-construction by the learner is an unconscious process which is best facilitated by bringing about in the learner a preoccupation with meaning, saying or doing.
>
> ibid.

The methodology comprised the pre-task and task stages, and some procedural guidance. The syllabus did not have any rigid format. It helped to provide guidelines for developing tasks.

The pre-task was a teacher-guided, whole-class activity. It served to orient the learners to solve the task on their own through a similar process of reasoning in similar situations, sets of facts, or texts.

A task meant a self-reliant activity by the learners (for five or ten minutes or longer, but without the teacher intervening) in which they perceived a particular goal to be achieved, knew what was to be done, and attempted it seriously, whether they succeeded or not.

The right kind of task required a reasonable challenge in it, neither too high nor too low. The challenge was considered too low if the task was too easy and the learner did not get a sense of achievement. The challenge would be considered too high if the learner knew from the beginning that there was no chance of success. Therefore, the ideal task was one where learners aspired for success and knew they could achieve it.

Each task, however, required an independent effort of the mind; that is, it was not possible to transfer either the outcome or the procedures of one mechanically to the other:

> The pattern is roughly analogous to that of a lesson in mathematics, where a problem is worked out publicly and a similar problem is then set for learners to work out on their own.
>
> ibid.

In their use of language, learners had to cope as well as they could to do the task-based activities. They could use single words, gestures or quote from the blackboard or the written sheet which stated the task. Sometimes they had to formulate alternative responses and simply choose one of them, seek suggestions from a peer or, as a last resort, use the mother tongue.

Learner response was not judged merely for its linguistic accuracy. If a learner used an expression incorrectly, she/he was corrected only incidentally and not by systematic drilling, etc. What was reckoned as learning on the part of learners was their spontaneous response, that is, the language used by them naturally without consciously thinking of linguistic patterns.

Sample tasks

On the next few pages are three tasks used during the project for class 8.

CTP LESSON: 30 January 1981

(The following is written on the blackboard.)

Mr George
09.15 a.m. : leaves home
09.45 a.m. : arrives at the office
10.45 a.m. : goes to the court
03.30 p.m. : returns to the office
05.30 p.m. : leaves the office
06.00 p.m. : arrives home

Mrs George
09.45 a.m. : leaves home
10.00 a.m. : arrives at the college
12.30 p.m. : leaves the college
12.45 p.m. : arrives home
01.45 p.m. : leaves home
02.00 p.m. : arrives at the college
04.30 p.m. : leaves the college
04.45 p.m. : arrives home

PRE-TASK

(Questions, which are deliberately varied in form, are as follows.)

1. Where is Mr George at 10.00 a.m.?
2. Who leaves home first in the morning?
3. When does Mrs George arrive at the college in the afternoon?
4. How long does Mrs George take to go from home to the college?
5. Who is at home at 1.00 p.m.?
6. How much time does Mr George spend at his office in the morning?

TASK

1. Who comes home last in the evening?
2. Where is Mrs George at 1.30 p.m.?
3. How much time does Mrs George spend at college in the morning?
4. When does Mrs George leave the college in the afternoon?
5. Who is at home at 9.30 a.m.?
6. Where is Mr George at 4.30 p.m.?
7. How much time does Mr George spend in his office in the afternoon?
8. Who does not come home for lunch?

CTP LESSON: 9 November 1981

(The first lesson on school timetables)

TIMETABLE: CLASS 8D

	09.30–10.15	10.15–11.00	11.00–11.45	11.45–12.30	02.00–02.45	02.45–03.30
Mon	Kannada	English	Maths	Science	History	Games
Tue	Maths	Geography	Drawing	Kannada	English	Debate

Wed	English	Science	History	Kannada	Maths	Geography
Thu	Kannada	English	Maths	Science	History	Drawing
Fri	Maths	Geography	Drawing	Kannada	English	Games
Sat	English	Science	History	Maths	Kannada	—

PRE-TASK

1. How many periods are there: every day/in the morning/in the afternoon?
2. When do classes begin/end in the morning/afternoon?
3. When is the lunch break?
4. When does the third/fifth/last period begin/end?
5. What does the class do in the first/third/last period on Tuesday/Friday?
6. What does the class do at 10.00/11.30/12.30/3.00?
7. How many periods are there in the whole week for English/History?
8. Kumar, a student of this class, wants to take a day's leave. But he does not want to miss his mathematics class. When can he take leave?

TASK[5]

1. How many periods are there on Saturday?
2. When does the second period end?
3. When does the last period begin on Thursday?
4. What does the class do in the fourth period on Friday?
5. What does the class do in the fifth period on Monday?
6. What is the class doing at 12 o'clock on Wednesday?
7. What is the class doing at 3 o'clock on Tuesday?
8. How many periods are there in a week for geography?

CTP LESSON: 23 February 1982

(The sixth lesson on class timetables)

PRE-TASK

(The teacher puts up a blank weekly timetable—five days in the week, five periods a day—on the blackboard. He first invites learners to suggest or write the numbers of different periods and the names of different days in the relevant boxes. The class does this without any difficulty. Then the

[5] These questions are asked orally while the responses are given in the written form.

teacher makes the following statements and invites various learners to make appropriate entries in the timetable.)

1. The first period on Wednesday is English.
2. The second period on Tuesday is Tamil.
3. The last period on Thursday is maths.
4. The last period on Friday is history.
5. There is a lesson in English on Thursday in the third period.
6. There is a lesson in English on Monday in the third period.
7. On Wednesday, there is a lesson in maths just after English.
8. On Thursday, there is a maths lesson just before English.
9. The Tamil lesson on Friday is in the third period.
10. The first period on Tuesday is English.

TASK

(A blank timetable on paper—with the days and numbers of periods filled in—is then distributed to learners, who listen to the following set of statements and attempt to make the relevant entries.)

1. The second period on Wednesday is Tamil.
2. The third period on Monday is English.
3. There is a maths lesson in the last period on Thursday.
4. There is a lesson in history just after English on Monday.
5. The English lesson on Thursday is in the fourth period.

APPLICATION

Divide yourself into two groups A and B. Group A should make a list of the positive features of the communicational approach. Group B should prepare a list of the shortcomings/problems inherent in the communicational approach. Debate the points in class.

NEW PERSPECTIVES: THE LEXICAL APPROACH

The preceding chapters have shown how different schools of thought have influenced and shaped the approaches and methods in English language teaching. Certain ideas and concepts that appeared in the last two decades of the twentieth century have further shaped ELT in the areas of approach and syllabus design. One of these is the lexical approach, the outcome of the COBUILD dictionary project under the academic direction of John Sinclair. For perhaps the first time, a bank of computers at the University of Birmingham was used to collect and analyse a corpus of authentic English. This corpus was the basis of the COBUILD dictionary, and it consisted of samples of 'real' English,[6] that is, English as it is spoken and written by native speakers of English.

The collection of this corpus threw up patterns of English usage that people like Harold Palmer had discussed (but perhaps not developed). The patterns that emerged showed that the lexicon of English consisted of mainly multi-word items (and not just single words) of different types that collocated in a fairly fixed way or that occurred in fixed expressions such as the following:

MULTI-WORD ITEMS

1. polywords: *by the way, nevertheless*
2. arbitrary combinations: *black and white, to and fro*

COLLOCATIONS

1. fixed: *run a test*
2. fairly fixed (which permit a limited number of possibilities):

   strong
weak
black *coffee* (but not *powerful coffee* or *brown coffee*)
white

OTHER FIXED EXPRESSIONS

1. social language:
   How do you do?
   Happy Teachers' Day!
2. politeness phrases:
   Yes, please.
   No, thank you.
3. language used in specific contexts:
   Could you tell me the time, please?
   I'd like an orange.
4. idioms:
   The pot calling the kettle black
   Raining cats and dogs

---

[6] as opposed to plausible language constructs usually used in teaching and producing ELT materials

The corpus analysis of native speaker behaviour shows that 'not only are there interdependencies across lexical items that are not mediated by grammar, but that grammatical regularities are themselves dependent on the lexis they are associated with' (Howatt 1984). In other words, language use was found to be based more on lexis than on grammar, and on chunks of language rather than on single words. These findings had a direct bearing on what the content of language teaching should be and how language should be taught. The lexical approach articulates the principles underpinning it, the most important of which is:

> The heart of this approach is the communication of meaning. Only when learners have a sufficiently large mental lexicon can they use grammatical knowledge to manipulate language.
>
> ibid.

Pedagogical implications

The lexical approach can be summarised in a few words: language consists not of traditional grammar and vocabulary but often of multiword prefabricated chunks.

> Teachers using the Lexical Approach will, instead of analysing language wherever possible, be more inclined to direct learners' attention to chunks which are as large as possible.
>
> Lewis 1997

A common reaction of teachers to the lexical approach was to see it as something that replaced the grammatical syllabus. But proponents of the approach warned against such interpretations. Lewis is very emphatic:

> I totally disassociate myself from any suggestion that the 'Lexical Approach' denies the value of grammar, and … any suggestion that 'Lexis is the answer' …. Both explicitly contradict my belief in our dynamic, ever-evolving understanding of both language and learning.
>
> ibid.

What are the changes that the lexical approach suggests? It suggests a shift in focus:

- from sentence grammar to lexis (multi-word chunks)

- from talking for the sake of talking in L2 to listening (at lower levels) and reading (at higher levels)
- from indiscriminate recording of new words to the use of the dictionary as an active source of learning
- from uncollocated nouns to specific language areas

Methodology

The lexical approach does not have a specific methodology: most of its classroom transactions are based on tasks. The following quote from Lewis explains the stand taken by advocates of the approach:

> Several correspondents, attracted by the theoretical position set out in the Lexical Approach have written to ask 'What would a lexical lesson be like?', but, as we already emphasised, the Lexical Approach is not an all-embracing method, but a set of principles based on a new understanding of language .... [There are] two characteristics to all new or newly-focussed activities: firstly, attention is directed to larger chunks of language than has been the norm .... Secondly, activities tend to unify the teaching of grammar, lexis and pronunciation; a chunk may be taught as a lexical item, a phonological unit, and as grammatical input. These two principles—holistic and unifying—are applied in many different ways.
>
> ibid.

Think it over

Could there be any drawbacks in the use of the lexical approach in a second-language situation, such as in India?

Section summary

- The lexical approach emerged out of the COBUILD dictionary project.
- The lexical approach is based on the patterns of English usage that occur in 'chunks' in native-speaker English.
- In the lexical approach, the focus shifts from teaching structures/grammar to teaching vocabulary in context.
- Competence in using language to communicate meaning is the aim of the lexical approach.

Did you understand?

1. What, in your opinion, is the main factor that led to the development of the lexical approach?
2. Name the main types of language 'chunks' we find in English.
3. Does the use of the lexical approach mean that no grammar is taught? Explain.
4. Is the lexical approach different from the communicative approach? If yes, in what way(s)?

Application

Task 1

Study the tasks below and say which of them has an orientation towards the lexical approach, and which does not. Give reasons for your answer.

a. Match the following.

big	a writing instrument
bag	clever
sharp	huge
pencil	a container

b. Practise saying with the correct stress and intonation the following phrases that describe reactions. Use the phrases to talk about R.K. Narayan's story 'The Blind Dog'.

Phrase (i)	What I found (most)	shocking amusing interesting difficult	was
Phrase (ii)	I felt	sorry happy pity	for

Task 2

On the next page is part of a concordance list (a format that allows you to see the linguistic contexts before and after the word under study). How can you exploit it to teach grammar?

Mmm … no, I've never broken	*any*	bones so far … er, just some …
Certainly not me! I don't really get	*any*	colds, or … Well, I think I …
… that allows me to cope with almost	*any*	circumstances, and to make friends.
… are the worst paid. Do you think	*any*	of them is underpaid or overpaid?
… secretary's desk to see if there were	*any*	messages for him. There were none.
… but when it happened, I never had	*any*	reply. I had to just sit there.
… and healthy. I didn't really have	*any*	career ambitions. Er … partly because …
… penalty goes with which offence.	*Any*	comments, Sergeant Brown?
… door closed and locked and secure	*any*	ladders. Do always lock your …
He said, 'You don't. And you ain't.	*Any*	fool could tell that.' He took from …

NEW TRENDS: LANGUAGE TEACHING DESIGN

A significant development in the area of language teaching design is the Council of Europe's 'Common European Framework of Reference for Languages: Learning, Teaching, Assessment'—the CEFR, or CEF, for short. The CEF is a document of nine chapters and four appendices, and is available on the Council of Europe website: www.coe.int.

The CEF (p. 1) aims to

> … provide a common basis for the elaboration of language syllabuses, curriculum guidelines, examinations, textbooks, etc. across Europe. It describes in a comprehensive way what learners have to learn to do in order to use a language for communication, and what language and skills they have to develop so as to be able to act effectively …. The Framework also defines levels of proficiency which allows learners' progress to be measured at each stage of learning on a life-long basis.

The CEF is a descriptive document that lists out options available to the syllabus designer, the teacher, and the materials producer. Morrow (1981) identifies four core areas in the CEF.

1. *The learner:* The CEF analyses the factors that make up individual differences.
2. *The language:* A clear description of the content in terms of competencies a learner should acquire. The competencies are

(a) linguistic competency, which includes grammar, vocabulary, etc., and the capacity to use them; (b) sociolinguistic competency, the ability to identify and use language that is appropriate to a specific culture or group; (c) pragmatic competency, or understanding and using language effectively in interactions.

3. *Levels of performance:* The CEF has identified levels of learner proficiency in terms of descriptor scales. These descriptors are a series of 'can do' statements, and these have received a great deal of attention.
4. *Teaching and learning:* The CEF articulates its belief in learner involvement in the learning process, and the need for learners to take responsibility for their learning. It also sets out the thesis that teacher empowerment happens when teachers are reflective and can choose the options best suited for a situation.

Of all the sections of the CEF, the global scales have impacted very quickly and thoroughly one section of the language-learning process, namely, testing. The global scales are represented as follows:

A Basic user		B Independent user		C Proficient user	
A1	A2	B1	B2	C1	C2
Break through	Waystage	Threshold	Vantage	Effective operational efficiency	Mastery

The scales (also called the Common Scale of Reference) describe proficiency levels in reception, production, interaction and mediation. These are different from the LSRW usually used, and they focus on what the learner can do. Given below are examples of the highest and lowest levels of the scale.

C2 Can understand with ease virtually everything heard or read. Can summarise information from different spoken and written sources, reconstructing arguments and accounts in a coherent presentation. Can express himself/herself spontaneously, very fluently and precisely, differentiating finer shades of meaning even in more complex situations.

A1 Can understand and use familiar everyday expressions and very basic phrases aimed at the satisfaction of needs of a concrete type. Can introduce himself/herself and others, and can ask and answer questions about personal details, such as where he/she lives, people he/she knows, and things he/she has. Can interact in a simple way, provided the other person talks slowly and clearly and is prepared to help.

The impact of the CEF on proficiency examinations has by extension affected the production of books that aid learners to acquire the competencies required by these examinations. In the 1970s and 80s, the Council of Europe's 'Threshold Level' led to the development of the notional-functional syllabus and finally to the communicative approach.

The Language Policy Division has worked for forty years to produce this framework of reference. Case studies are being conducted on the impact of the CEF, and the CEF has been translated into Japanese. However, we will have to wait a few more years to see what changes in teaching and learning English as a second language will result from the CEF.

THINK IT OVER

1. What impact do you think the CEF will have on the teaching of English in India?
2. Do you think a similar study should be done and a framework evolved for the teaching of L2 in India? Do you think we can adopt the CEF totally? Why or why not?

Part II

This part deals with the various techniques of teaching language skills and the use of teaching aids. The final chapter on testing shows how we can evaluate ability, knowledge and performance.

6

Techniques of Teaching English

How a thing is done in class is a *technique.* A technique is 'implementational—that which actually takes place in a classroom. It is a particular trick, stratagem or contrivance used to accomplish an immediate objective' (Anthony 1972). Techniques are closely related to methods and approaches.

> Different theories about the nature of language and how languages are learned (the approach) imply different ways of teaching language (the method), and different methods make use of different kinds of classroom activity (techniques).
>
> *Longman Dictionary of Applied Linguistics* 1985

The objective in any language classroom is to get the learners to learn the target language and use it, which is done best when they are involved actively in the learning process. This in turn means that their interest must be sustained in classroom activity. A teacher who has a repertoire of techniques to teach different skills and sub-skills is more likely to succeed in this objective than one who has a limited number of techniques at command.

Another important point to be remembered is that having a repertoire of techniques is by itself no guarantee of success; one must know *when* to use *which* technique. In other words, the judgement of a teacher should be fine-tuned to the needs of that particular class or group of learners. For example, drilling is a technique which can be used effectively at the practice or familiarisation stage of a lesson, but not for a communicative activity which demands deployment of the learner's own language.

Language has been divided into four main skills, namely listening, speaking, reading and writing (LSRW). Each skill has been further divided into sub-skills.

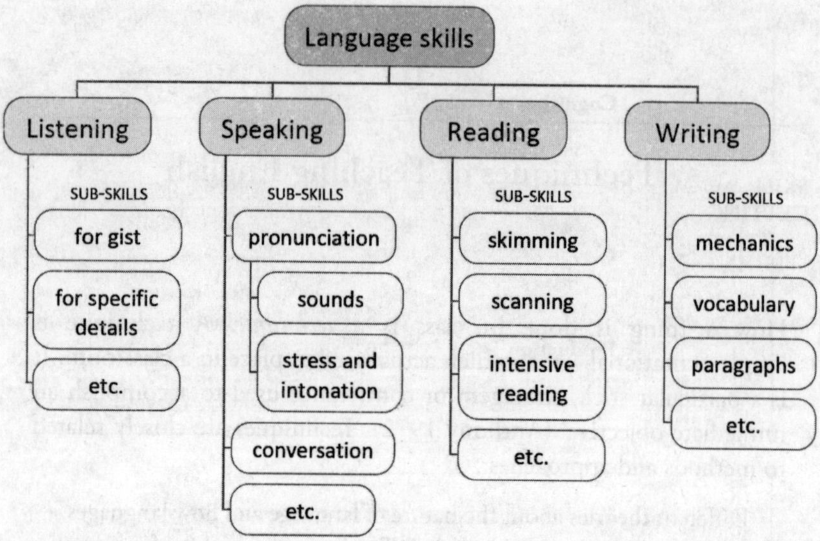

Think it over

Language has been divided into skills and sub-skills. But are these skills and sub-skills totally isolated from each other? Do we use only one skill/sub-skill at a time?

Before proceeding further, it would be useful here to quickly go over a proposition which was put forward by W.M. Rivers and M.S. Temperley in 1978. They proposed that the learning skills of a language fall into two main categories, one complementing the other (see the diagram on the next page).

You will notice that activities in the class tend to fall into either the *skill-getting* or *skill-using* category. It is important to remember that the techniques we use in a classroom should not stop at skill-getting activities but must extend to skill-using activities too.

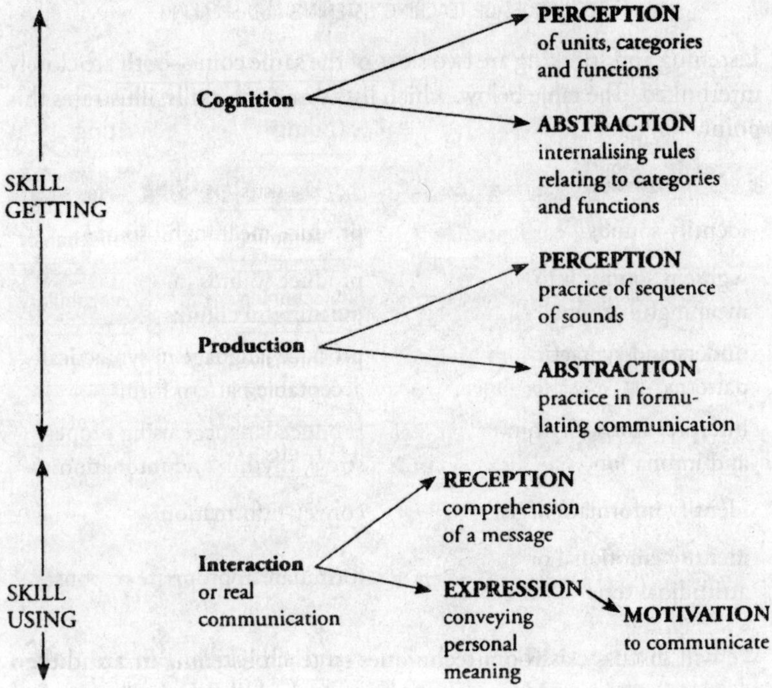

Rivers and Temperley 1978

THINK IT OVER

1. What sorts of activities were you exposed to in your school days while learning your mother tongue or English?
2. What were the techniques used by your teachers?

In this chapter, we will discuss different techniques which can be used for teaching different skills. Techniques which integrate these skills and sub-skills will also be given. Try to identify which of these techniques are skill-getting techniques and which are skill-using ones.

TECHNIQUES OF TEACHING LISTENING AND SPEAKING

Listening and speaking are two sides of the same coin—both are closely interlinked. The table below, which lists some sub-skills, illustrates this point.

Listening		Speaking
identify sounds	→	produce meaningful sounds
segment sounds into meaningful groups	→	produce sounds in meaningful chunks
understand syntactic patterns	→	produce language in syntactically acceptable pattern forms
interpret stress, rhythm and intonation	→	produce language using proper stress, rhythm and intonation
identify information/gist	→	convey information
identify emotional or attitudinal tone	→	formulate appropriate response

We will discuss classroom techniques to teach listening first and then go on to speaking. More than one skill/sub-skill may be involved in these activities, but the focus will be on listening/speaking.

Listening

A clear distinction must be made between *listening* and *hearing*. When we listen, we pay conscious attention to what is being said. A good listener learns a language quickly and efficiently. So, it is very important to think of techniques which will enable learners to listen better and more efficiently.

Count it

This technique can be used to get learners to identify the number of times a specific sound, word or grammatical category (for example, adjectives) occurs. The teacher plays a recording, or reads aloud (at normal speed) a short passage or a list of words. For example:

(The teacher says) Listen to the passage. You will hear it twice. The first time listen and write down the number of times you hear an adverb and a proper noun. Then, listen again and write down the number of times you hear the /d/ sound.

(Reads passage aloud) Somu came out of his daydream suddenly. He realised what had happened. He had lost all the milk through his own fault. Not a drop was left in the bucket. He picked it up sadly and returned home. Not only did the vision of him becoming rich vanish but he had to go home empty-handed without earning a single paisa. Somu learnt a valuable lesson that day—not to build castles in the air.

The learners draw a small grid in their notebooks at the beginning of the task. A sample grid for the above example is given below.

adverb	
proper noun	
/d/	

IDENTIFY IT

Words with contrasting sounds are read in isolation, and learners have to say what the sound is. The number of times the sound occurs is noted, and answers checked later. For example:

Teacher says	Learner notes down	Answers checked
vine	/v/	✓
wine	/w/	✓
wine	/v/	×
vine	/w/	×
wine	/w/	✓

Instead of isolated words, sentences can also be used. For example:

The vines/wines of France are famous.

The fan/van is not moving.

The pin/bin is too small.

WHAT IS IT?

The teacher puts up two pictures, or draws two pictures on the blackboard. A list of words is also put up. As the teacher says the words aloud, the class has to choose words which have the same sounds as the object of the pictures. For example:

ship

sheep

Word list: tip team seep beat deed

Learners then say the words aloud. Sounds which are difficult for the class can be identified. For example: /p/ and /f/, /θ/ and /t/, /aɪ/ and /eɪ/.

THINK IT OVER

What skills/sub-skills are the activities above focusing on?

LISTEN AND MARK/WRITE

Learners are asked to copy simple figures from the blackboard. The teacher reads out sentences, and the learners have to correctly write/tick/mark/identify, as per the instructions. For example:

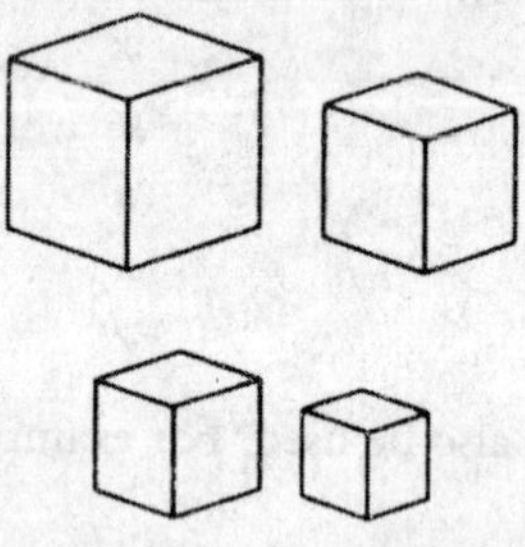

(The teacher says) Mark the boxes with the right colours.
The green box is the biggest.
The blue box is big, but the yellow box is bigger than the blue box.
The black box is the smallest.

GRID

Grids can be used at various levels. At the elementary stage, the teacher reads out just two or three sentences, and learners fill the grid. The example below illustrates how learners listen to a text and put a cross or a tick in each box of a grid.

(The teacher says or plays an audio recording) Ravi and Raju study in class 9. Ravi likes his school subjects and loves studying, but he hates games. Raju, on the other hand, loves playing kho kho and kabaddi. He likes English but cannot stand maths.

	Maths	English	Games
Ravi	✓	✓	×
Raju	×	✓	✓

A more complicated text can be used at an advanced stage. For example:

Well, we have neighbours. All of us do, I think. Mmm... let's see. On our left we have the Rao family. They bought their site way back in 1958. Quite a big one actually. The Singhs, on our right, bought theirs only in 1980. Paid a lot too. Opposite us? Well, no houses, only a park. Mr Singh employed a Mumbai architect and built a beautiful house on a smaller site. You know, modern and mmm... eye-catching. Mr Rao's house is traditional. Good, of course. A well in the backyard... banana trees... you know. No landscaping, like our other neighbour...

	Rao	Singh
Site bought in		
Money paid		
Type of house		
Type of garden		

This technique can be used for different text types, including semi-scientific ones and stories.

FAMILY TREE

A different type of graphic representation commonly used is the family tree. This can be drawn on the blackboard for learners to copy into their notebooks. The learners listen to the audio or the teacher, and fill in whatever is asked for in the task (for example, names). The text can be simple:

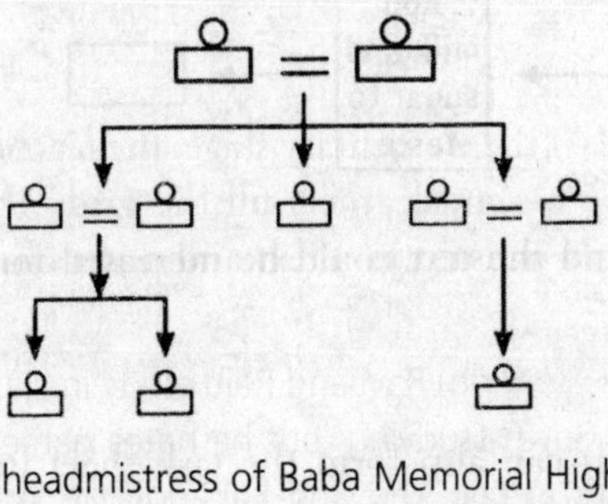

Bhim Joshi married Gouri in 1932. They had three children—two girls, Savita and Radha, and a boy, Nitin. Savita married Dalpat Rao. It was an arranged marriage. They have two children, Rohini and Abhishek. Radha did not marry at all. She is now the headmistress of Baba Memorial High School. Nitin married Kanchi, a girl from Nepal. They have a daughter, Shanti.

The text could be made more difficult:

I am Shanti. I have two aunts, Savita and Radha. Aunt Savita…

TIMETABLES, BIO-DATA FORMS, PASSPORT/BANK FORMS

These can all be used to give practice in and to test listening skills. A text can be read out and the learner asked to fill in details. Alternatively, there could be a conversation between two persons (for example, a bank manager and a client wishing to open an account, or a passport officer and a traveller) and the learners could be asked to fill in the relevant details.

FLOWCHARTS

These too can be used as a task sheet for a listening activity. Again, the input could be a text or a conversation. For example, the text could be about how to make tea. Learners first copy the flowchart with blanks in their notebooks. Then they listen to what is said and fill in the blanks. Look at the example below.

Take a kettle. Fill it with water.
Light the stove and boil the water.
Then add the boiling water to tea leaves.
After some time, strain the decoction.
Add milk and sugar to taste. Serve the tea hot.

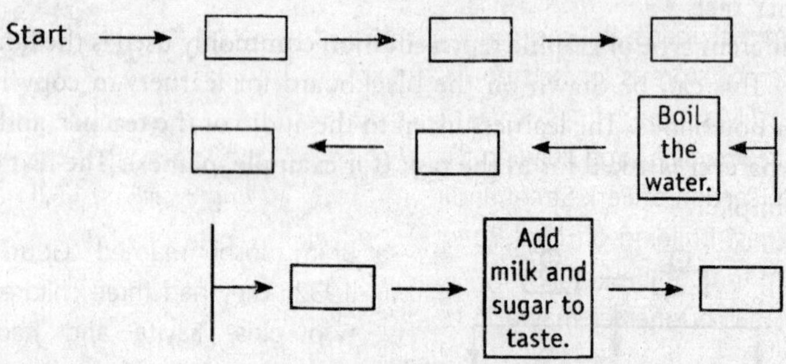

The complexity of the flowchart and the text could be increased for higher levels.

MAPS

Maps (either blank or partly filled) can also form the task sheet in listening activities. They can be used to mark a route, locate a particular place, or locate where different places are or where different people live. The input for these would again vary in complexity to suit the level of the learners.

Example 1

Zoya lives in MIG colony. Her house faces a lane leading to the main road. She left home at 8 a.m. to go to the market. She turned right on the lane as soon as she left the house. She did not want to take the footpath behind her house as the rains had made the path wet and muddy.

She walked along the lane and turned right on reaching the junction with the main road. She walked past the shops on the main road, and, after crossing the park, she turned right again and went straight. She avoided the shortcut through the park.

Mark Zoya's route to the market on the map.

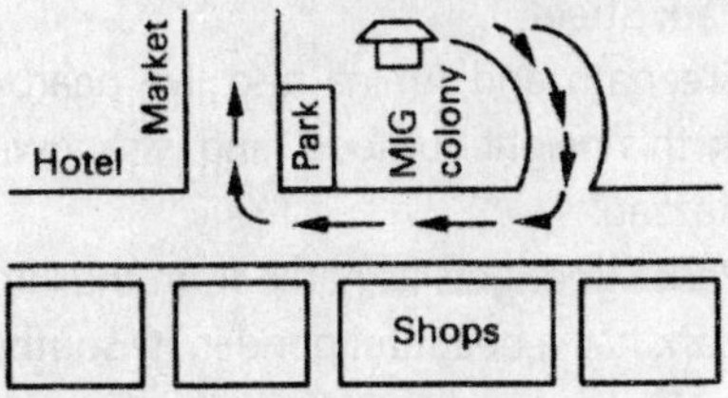

Example 2

This is a more difficult task which requires a lot of concentration on the part or the learner.

Instructions to learners: Copy the map into your notebook. Mark locations on the map based on what you hear.

(The teacher reads aloud or plays an audio recording) The Food Basket department store is located on Mall Road, between Regent Tower and the Plaza Mall.

Regent Tower is a large building that houses many offices. It is situated at the intersection of Park Street and Mall Road.

The largest building on Mall Road is the Plaza Mall shopping complex, adjacent to Food Basket.

Many small businesses may also be found on Mall Road, opposite Plaza Mall.

Facing Mall Road is a Chettinad restaurant and, beside it, a small café. The café sits on the corner of Mall Road and Hyder Ali Lane.

Directly opposite the café, on the other side of Hyder Ali Lane, is Namrata's grocery store.

Next to the grocery store are a hardware store and a pharmacy.

The pharmacy is owned by Ishita, who lives in the house facing the pharmacy. Between Ishita's house and the café is a florist's shop.

The large, L-shaped building nearby is Nanak High School, located on Park Street.

Aditi lives beside the school.

A car showroom is located on Park Street. It faces the west gate of Nanak High School.

Near the car showroom, are a cluster of houses.

Shiny lives in the big house behind the showroom. Her house has a swimming pool!

Razzaq lives in the house at the busy crossroad where Mall Road meets Park Street.

Sreenath and Amina also live nearby. Sreenath's house is the smallest in this neighbourhood, and is sandwiched between those of Amina and Razzaq.

Park Street gets its name from the large park opposite Regent Tower. The park has a beautiful pond in its southeastern corner.

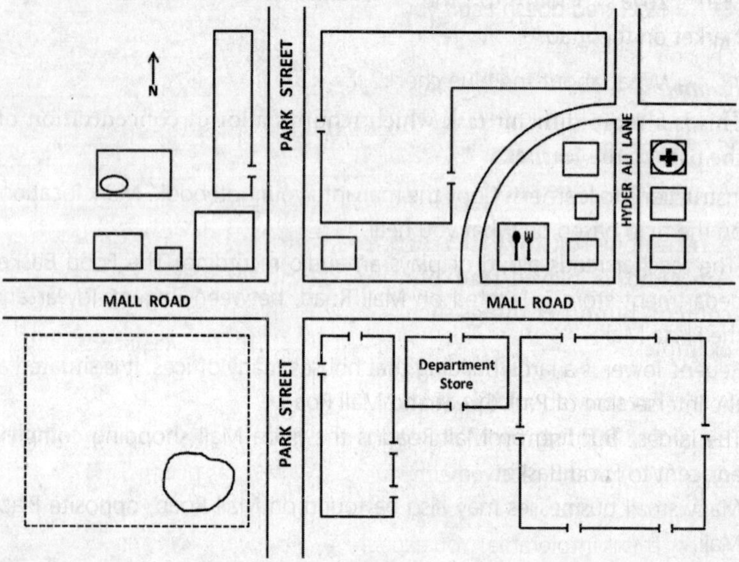

Think it over

1. Can you list at least three sub-skills that the activities above focus on?
2. Does it require any other knowledge besides that of the English language to do these activities?

STORIES/PASSAGES

These can be used to get the learners to listen to a gist. A set of titles are given and the learners are asked to match what they read to the title. For example:

Exercise regularly, follow a balanced diet, and do something nice for someone. That's the advice you may soon get from your doctor. An explosion of new research is pointing to the benefits of altruism.

Choice of titles:
Exercise is good
Eat well, live long
The power of goodness

Paragraph summaries too can be given as alternative input. The other technique is to give short conversations and ask learners to guess who is speaking, to whom and where. For example:

A I like the red one.
B No... red doesn't suit you.
A But I like it.
B What about the blue check?
A Oh, yes! It's lovely!... Oh, no...
B What's the matter?
A Look at the price!

A TECHNIQUE FOR ADVANCE LEVEL LEARNERS

An audio is played/read out, and questions asked not about the content, but other things such as mood, attitude and social status. For example:

A I'm sorry about this, sir, but...
B Oh! But I sent you a telegram and a letter.
A We haven't received either. And so, I'm sorry, but there is no room and... err...
B This is intolerable! You expect me to go and look for a room now?
A Well, I did tell you, sir, there's a wedding party and...
B I want to talk to the manager. Where is he?

The questions could be:

Who are the speakers?
Where is the conversation taking place?
Is it a friendly conversation?

What do you think has happened?
What words or phrases give you clues?
How would you describe the mood of the speakers?

Objective-type questions

One technique, or rather task type, which can be used for listening comprehension is to have learners first listen to a passage and then answer true/false or multiple-choice questions. The questions should be set carefully or else there will be no challenge involved in the listening activity.

Speaking

Naming objects

The best technique to learn to articulate meaningful sounds in a foreign or second language is to begin naming familiar objects around us. It is a pedagogic truth that this activity is very close to the way one learns any language. It is a fact that we may know and use an object without necessarily knowing its name in the target language. The teacher shows objects or pictures of common objects, and learners name the objects. For example:

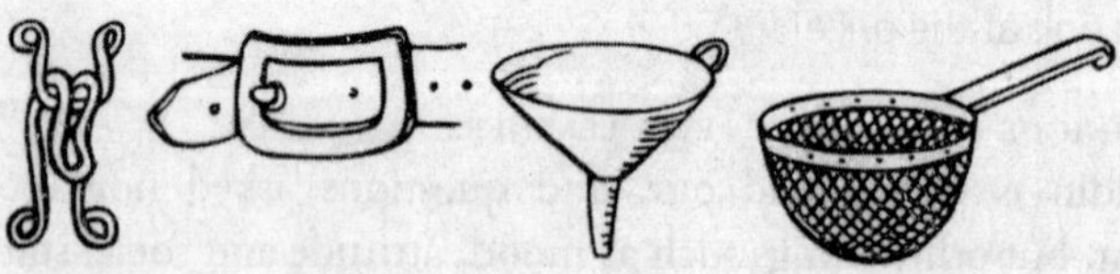

The class learns the word(s). Practice in saying these words can be offered individually or in chorus. A chart can be put up in the classroom where all the new words learnt are written. At the end of a week or a fortnight, the teacher can do a brief revision exercise.

hook and eye
belt buckle
funnel
sieve

Rhymes, chants and tongue-twisters

A very enjoyable way of learning to say English words and sentences is through rhymes and chants. Children in the primary and upper primary classes enjoy repeating rhymes. In addition to common nursery rhymes, short rhymes of various kinds can be used.

At a slightly advanced level, tongue-twisters can be used to practise difficult English sounds, or sounds which learners cannot articulate easily. The following tongue-twisters contrast the /s/ and /ʃ/ (sh) sounds, which are often a problem to our learners:

She sells sea-shells on the sea-shore.
But the sea-shells that she sells
Are not sea-shells of that shore.

The sixth sick Sheikh's
sixth sheep is sick.

BACK-CHAINING

For learners who cannot manage even a short unit of discourse, the back-chaining technique should be used. Look at the example below.

Teacher a book
Learner a book
Teacher reading a book
Learner reading a book
Teacher is reading a book
Learner is reading a book
Teacher The man is reading a book.
Learner The man is reading a book.

Incidentally, sentence stress can be acquired by learners through this activity.

QUESTIONS AND ANSWERS

In most of our classes, it is the teacher who asks questions and expects quick answers. The activities in this section help learners to both answer and ask questions.

Activity 1: Questions based on visuals

At the elementary level, a visual is displayed which encourages learners to answer questions and also ask questions to other learners. The teacher asks some questions based on the visual, and learners are required to give short answers to the questions.[1]

[1] Our learners are often taught to answer in full sentences to a simple question like 'What's your name?'.

Question	How many people are there in the picture?
Answer	Three.
Question	What is the man doing?
Answer	Reading.
Question	Is he reading a newspaper?
Answer	No, he isn't. He is reading a book.
Question	What is the boy doing?
Answer	Playing with the dog.
Question	Isn't he playing with the girl?
Answer	No, he isn't.
Question	Is he happy?
Answer	Yes, he is.
Question	Where is the girl?
Answer	On a swing.

This technique can be used at the practice stage. It can also be used in an information-gap exercise communicatively. In pairs, one learner asks questions about a picture that the second learner has, and the first learner draws the same picture based on the information she/he can elicit. The picture is then compared with the original. These are known as *information-gap activities*.

Activity 2: Picture cards

Two sets of picture cards are needed for this activity. The cards can be as follows:

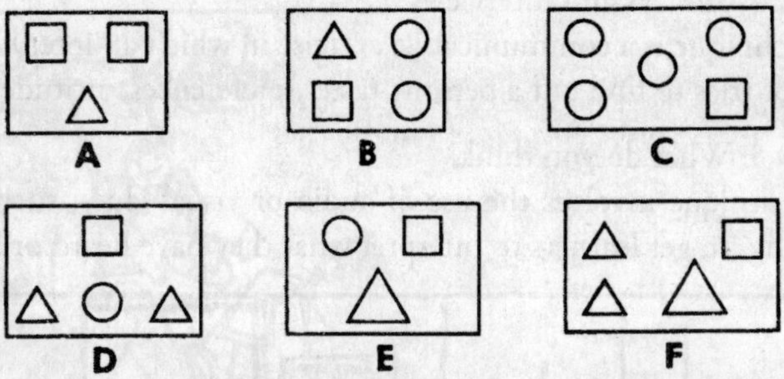

The cards are distributed among groups of learners in the class. (Ideally, the group should consist of four or five learners. If the class is large, more cards may have to be made.) The teacher has a card which matches one of the learners' cards. Each learner asks some questions of the following kinds (both 'wh–' and 'yes/no') to find out if his/her card matches the teacher's card:

How many triangles are there?
Does your card have a square in it?

The same cards can be used for pair work in the following manner. A learner has a 'master' sheet and a number of cards. His/her partner has only one of these cards. The first learner asks questions such as those below to find out which of his/her cards matches his/her partner's card.

Does your card have a square on it?
Does it have a triangle?
Is the triangle big or small?
Where is the triangle?
Is there a small square on the top right corner?
Is there a circle on the top left corner?

The answers to the questions will help the learner say, for example:

You have card E.

After the answer is checked, learners exchange roles (with a different card).

Activity 3: The twenty-question game

In this game, learners ask 'yes/no' questions to find out the object/person the teacher has thought of.

Activity 4: Surveys and interviews

This technique is a communicative exercise in which an interviewer or surveyor tries to find out a person's tastes, preferences, attitudes, etc.

Activity 5: What do you think?

This technique involves the use of audio or visual clues, such as the following, to get learners to interpret what they have heard or seen.

First, questions about visual comprehension can be asked.

What is the man doing?
What does the man have with him?
Is the door open or shut?
Is the man happy or unhappy?

These can be followed by questions that require interpretation.

Why do you think the man is unhappy?
How long do you think has he been sitting on the step?
Why isn't he inside the house?
Whose house is it? How do you know?

Learners may answer in a word or two, or even in the mother tongue in the beginning. Do not let that worry you. They will have begun to communicate what they think. Help with the language. Remember that in such activities there is no one correct answer.

DIALOGUES AND ROLE PLAY

These techniques deal with the interactional aspect of speaking. Some of the techniques commonly used are outlined in the next couple of pages.

Dialogue chains can be used to practise functions of language such as greeting, agreeing, disagreeing, and asking for information and suggestions.

Hello.	Hello.
What's your name?	Nisha.
In which class are you studying?	7-A. And you?
Class 7-D. Are you new here?	Yes, I joined yesterday.
Will you be my friend?	Thank you, yes.
Shall we go to the playground?	Let's.

Later, clues can be given and dialogues improvised. Learners can try their own innovations too. For example:

You are waiting for your friend outside a cinema. Your friend arrives a few minutes late.

Friend	(greets)
You	(return greeting)
Friend	(apologises for being late)
You	(accept apology; ask reason)
Friend	(gives reasons)
You	(suggest going in)
Friend	(agrees)

The clues can be for pairs or small groups of 3–4 learners. Places such as a restaurant, a school library, a karate class, or a friend's house may be chosen. The situations should be real and plausible—learners should feel that they *might* be in such a situation. Aspects of appropriacy[2] as well as accuracy are taken care of in such activities.

Role play is a popular technique used in classes to teach speaking skills. There are three kinds of role play.

1. Totally controlled: The roles are written out and the learners have to just speak the lines. For example, an exchange between a shopkeeper and a customer may be tried out in this way.
2. Clued: Here, linguistic and content clues are provided. For example, a clued role-play card would read as follows:

---

[2] appropriacy: the suitability of an utterance produced by a speaker for a particular situation and audience

place	bus station
characters	booking clerk and traveller
role play	A traveller wants to buy a ticket to Mumbai on a super deluxe bus. He wants to know the fare, time of departure, time of arrival, etc.
language you might need	Could you tell me…, What time…, Will it…, etc.

3. Free: Here only the roles or characters are given and learners have to develop the exchange in a suitable situation. Alternatively, characters are given in a particular situation and learners have to develop the exchange appropriate to it. For example:

A manager and a worker in a factory
A doctor and a policeman on a traffic island
An emergency operation in a theatre (three people)
An examination hall in a curfew-bound area (five people)

Problems

These are a good source for making learners speak. The learners will be engaged in grappling with a problem, and they will need to use language to solve it. For example:

Ahmed was over seventy years old. He had three sons. Ali was the eldest, Bashir was the second son, and Samir was the youngest. Ahmed did not have much money, but he had seventeen beautiful camels. Before he died, he said to Ali, 'You are my eldest son; you will have half of all my camels. He said to Bashir, 'You are my second son; you shall have a third of all my camels.' He said to Samir, 'You are my youngest son; you will have one-ninth of all my camels.'
Question: How did the sons divide the camels?
Answer: The Sheikh had a white camel which he gave to the three brothers. That made 18 camels. He told the brothers to divide the camels, but not take his white one.
1/2 of 18 = 9 camels; 1/3 of 18 = 6 camels; 1/9 of 18 = 2 camels
The Sheikh took back his camel.

There are other problems like the one given above.

A man has to cross a stream in a boat which can take only two persons or things at a time. The man has a goat, a tiger and a bundle of hay. How does he cross the stream?

OPINIONS

When opinions are asked for, especially on controversial topics or situations, a lot of discussion can be generated, and learners will use language to communicate. Here are some examples of ethical issues that may be discussed in class.

Your grandmother, who is old and very fond of you, makes a dish of milk sweets for you. You tell your grandmother that the dish is delicious, even though you hate milk sweets. Are you a liar?

You see a close friend of yours stealing a pen from a classmate's bag. The classmate complains to the teacher. The teacher asks the class if they know anything about it. What do you do?

EXPERIENCES

Learners can be encouraged from the primary classes to relate their experiences, however simple or ordinary. This is a step towards mastering communicative skills. For example:

What did you do on Sunday?

Thomas, you were ill for two days. Could you tell us what happened, please.

Renu, you went to Chennai for your cousin's wedding. We would like to hear about your experiences on the train and at the wedding.

DREAMS

All of us like to talk about our ambitions and dreams. This activity is open-ended and can lead to a lot of speaking. Visuals can be used as input in the early stages. For example:

Look at the above pictures and say what you would like to become.

Other questions that can be asked include:
Where would you like to go?
What would you like to buy?

Ideas and suggestions

Learners may be given ideas and topics for discussion; for example, 'How I would make things better'. This title can cover different things, from school amenities to municipal work to administering a country. Young learners could be motivated by showing them children's pages in the daily newspapers. It would, incidentally, make the learner feel that a young person's opinion is respected enough to be published.

Application

Task 1

Can you find similarities between the listening and speaking techniques given in this section? (The table at the beginning of the chapter should help you.)

Task 2

What input materials do you think are most necessary for listening/speaking?

Task 3

What listening/speaking tasks would you choose for class 7 children living in an entirely rural environment? Why?

TECHNIQUES OF TEACHING READING AND WRITING

While discussing reading and writing, it is usual to talk of levels. This is because the sub-skills involved in both these have to be clearly spelt out. The figure below illustrates this in brief.

Reading		Writing
learning to recognise letters/words/sentences	→	learning to form letters
understanding conventions used in graphic representations of language	→	learning punctuation skills
learning the meaning of written words	→	learning to write words

learning to 'chunk' sentences into sense groups and interpreting them	→	learning to write phrases/ sentences
understanding and interpreting discourse	→	producing written discourse

To equip learners to read and write, certain pre-reading and pre-writing tasks are suggested. The use of these tasks gives learners 'reading readiness' and 'writing readiness'. These techniques are usually used at the pre-primary level. For example, some of these pre-reading/ pre-writing activities require learners to match similar shapes, trace or copy out shapes, find the odd one out, etc.

Reading

Before discussing reading comprehension, it would be worthwhile to understand

- *why* a person reads, or the 'purpose'
- *how* a person reads, or 'method', which is related to the purpose
- *what* a person reads, or 'materials', which is in turn related to the purpose and the method

The following table shows the interrelationship between the three.

Why?	How?	What?
to get the gist	skim	newspapers, magazines, articles, etc.
to get a particular bit of information	scan	telephone directory, exam results, television or train schedules, lottery results, etc.
to understand completely what the writer is saying, and to evaluate a text	in-depth reading	research papers, professional articles, journals, etc.

Some specialists make a distinction between scanning for a particular bit of information and reading for the central idea. The latter, they argue, requires a more detailed reading than scanning. Since all of us need to acquire all three types of reading sub-skills, our techniques should aim at teaching our children different types of reading.

Mechanics of reading

Given below are some reading-readiness tasks, which deal with the mechanics of reading.

Matching shapes

Since reading consists of deciphering shapes, these activities at the initial level help learners to master the shapes of the English alphabet. They can be conducted in two ways.

Method 1

The learner matches the cut-outs of shapes given to him.

Usually, these shapes are cut out of fairly thick cardboard and are either coloured or covered with glazed paper. A number of these shapes are placed on the table and learners try to match them.

Method 2

Shapes are drawn in two parallel lines, and learners asked to draw a line joining similar shapes.

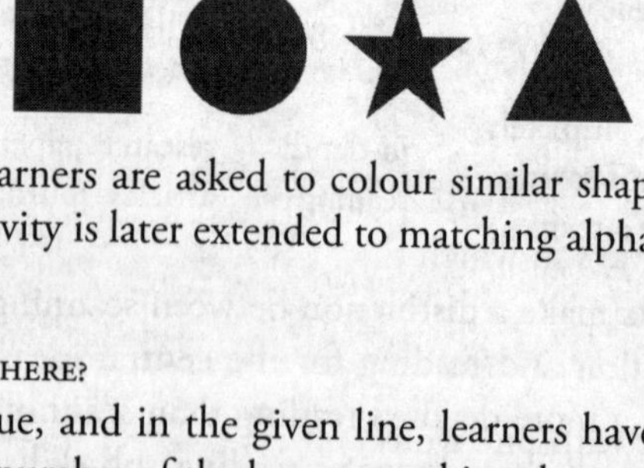

Alternatively, learners are asked to colour similar shapes in the same colour. This activity is later extended to matching alphabets, using the same technique.

How many are there?

A letter is the cue, and in the given line, learners have to count and write down the number of the letters matching the cue. For example:

c a c d g o o c c q o o

d d g j d d b b g q t d d b b d

Later, simple words are given, and learners have to write down the words beginning with the cue letter.

s	ship	sheep	zoo	pass	rose	
b	dog	god	boy	rub	dub	bud

TRACING/COPYING OUT SHAPES

When we are not sure of the spelling of a word, we write it out. That is because our visual memory of words is usually quite strong. When children copy out letters, they are strengthening this visual memory. Although this could be classified as a strictly writing activity, its advantages are seen when children start learning to read.

DISCRIMINATION

A set of letters/words are given and learners have to either circle the odd letter/word or copy it out.

a o a a a a

cry cry cry cry cray cry

The number of words a reader can take in at a time is called the eye-span. To begin with, our eye moves from word to word. Later, this increases to several words at a time. Reading speed, which is closely related to this skill of taking in chunks of words, can be improved using various techniques in the initial years. The chunking that a good reader does is not random, but is based on sense groups. For example, a good reader will chunk the sentence below in the following way:

Sarvesh is about forty-five / and his hair / is starting to go grey.

not:

Sarvesh is / about forty-five / and his / hair is / starting to / go grey.

A couple of ways in which the chunking skill can be developed are suggested below.

Command cards

The cards begin with one word and extend up to a sentence (see the examples on the next page). They are held up for just five seconds, and learners have to read them and carry out the commands. The teacher does not speak.

Sit.	Stand up.

Go to the door.

Go to the door and come back.

Touch your neighbour's hair.

Texts

These can be written in chunks, using proper sense groups. Learners read these passages (usually stories) and then re-tell them. For example:

Once upon a time / there was a billy-goat / who drew a little goat-carriage / on the sea-sands. / But one day / when he was getting old / he became lame.

The story is written out in chunks on a display board or on chart paper, and the teacher reveals the story (if it is short) chunk by chunk; or, she/he gives the story to the children using strips of cardboard on which the chunks are written. The activity should be performed briskly. An important thing to remember here is to grade the stories from simple five-sentence ones to longer ones, depending on the level of the class.

Techniques to teach reading skills

A variety of techniques can be used to train the learner in the different sub-skills of skimming, scanning and intensive reading.

SKIMMING

Skimming is closely related to the speed of reading. Students must learn to run their eyes quickly through the given material. The following techniques are effective in providing practice in skimming.

Finding the right word

Learners go through texts (such as the following) very quickly (say, one or two seconds for each sentence) and tick the answer.

All goods purchased at this shop must be paid for in [clash, cash].
The [whether, weather] will remain dry and sunny.

At the primary and middle school levels, the teacher can make 'sentence cards' with the relevant words deleted. These deleted words are put up on the blackboard. The teacher holds up each card for a few seconds and puts them face-down on the table.

Words on the blackboard:

god	dog	(mirror image problem)
cuboard	cupboard	(spelling + pronunciation)
bare	bear	(homophones)

Sentence cards:

We pray to .... every day.

The old woman's .... was bare.

I can't .... to see blood.

How many times?

This activity can be done using cardboard strips, on each of which a key word appears one or more times together with misspelt words very close to the key word. The key words are written on the blackboard. Learners run their eyes quickly over the strips and say how many times a key word occurs in each of them. Look at the examples below.

laughter	**laughter laughter lahfter laughter**
round	**ruond round rond ruond**
ceiling	**cieling ceiling cieling ceiling**

Matching titles to texts

A short text (such as a paragraph from the English reader) is given, and learners are asked to skim through quickly and choose the appropriate title. Look at the examples below.

One student asked her friend, 'Have you read any mysteries lately?'
'Yes', her friend said, 'I'm reading one now.'
'What's the title?'
'*Advanced Algebra*.'

Tick the appropriate title for the above text.

a. Mystery Stories
b. Mathemystery
c. Advanced Algebra

Generally when we speak of ice, we have only two kinds of ice in mind: one, which is obtained by freezing water and which we add to cold drinks, and the other, the snow that falls in the mountains during winter. Both of these are formed by the condensation of water. But there is also a third kind of ice, which is called 'dry ice'. Unlike ordinary ice, this is not made from water. On the contrary, it is prepared from carbon dioxide.

Tick the appropriate title for the above text.

a. Dry Ice
b. Ice-making
c. Types of Ice

The titles should not have subtle differences. Then, only a detailed read will help the learners choose the right title.

Matching pictures to texts
The activity is another way of teaching learners to skim through texts. For example:

Match the following descriptions with the right pictures.

Gog has a round body and a round head.
Cog has a round head and a square body.
Hog has a square body and a square head.

Matching diagrams and texts
Diagrams and texts are given and they must be matched. A variation of this technique is to give one diagram and many texts, or vice versa, and ask learners to match the right ones.

Matching topics and texts
A short text and a list of topics are given, and learners are required to match the text with its topic. Newspaper items can be used as input material for this activity.

SCANNING

Scanning is a sub-skill that allows the reader to find a particular piece of information in a text. The following activities will train learners in acquiring and improving the ability to scan texts for specific details.

Activity 1

An extract from a directory is given and learners are asked to find, for example:

- the telephone number of a person whose name is given
- the pin code of the area
- the address of a person

Activity 2

An extract from a dictionary is given and the following task is set.

interest a. a readiness to give attention: I have no interest in politics.
b. an activity, subject, etc., which one gives time and attention to: Eating seems to be his only interest in life.
c. money paid for the use of money: He lent me the money at 6% interest.

What does 'interest' mean in the following sentences?

1. She looks after her own interests.
2. This subject has no interest for me.
3. Interest rates have been cut by half percent.
4. Social work is one of her interests.
5. The dog returned his kindness with interest.

If it is difficult to get a dictionary extract, the teacher can prepare a few charts with words and their various meanings (not in the dictionary style), or verbs/phrasal verbs and their various meanings, and ask learners to match the use of the words in given sentences with their meanings.[3] For example:

make up a. to invent something (a story, a poem, an excuse)
b. to apply cosmetics on the face to improve appearance
c. to prepare, arrange or put together
d. to compensate for work that was missed
e. to constitute; to form something
f. to become friends again (after a quarrel)

[3] Always provide a context for the word as the word gets its meaning from its context.

1. Water is made up of oxygen and hydrogen.
2. He was made up and put in front of the camera.
3. It's time you made up with your partner.
4. That child makes up the most incredible stories.
5. She was told to make up for the week she spent in the hospital.
6. I will make up a bed for you in the drawing room.

Activity 3

Instructions on how to use a piece of equipment (a washing machine, a pump set, etc.), how to purify water, fire-safety rules, and other such materials can be used to frame scanning exercises, such as the following:

- True/false questions can be given, and learners asked to check against the instructions.
- Statements are given, and learners should say which rule or instruction they are based on.

Activity 4

The learner is asked to read an extract from a text, such as a paragraph of a lesson in the prescribed reader, and to answer scanning questions based on it. Look at the examples below.

When did Hillary and Tenzing reach Base Camp III?
When was the Red Cross Society founded?
How many times does the word 'music' occur in the passage? (It could even be words like 'must', 'this', or 'so'.)

Activity 5

The index or content page of the textbook can be used and the following type of questions asked.

On which page is the poem 'The Wonderful World'?
On which pages does the word 'discovery' occur?
In which lesson do you find the structure 'I would… if I could'?

Speed is the most important factor in skimming and scanning exercises. The teacher can organise class competitions to motivate learners to read quickly.

INTENSIVE/IN-DEPTH READING

The type of questions determine the type or depth of reading required. Judiciously prepared questions can lead a learner to interact productively and actively with a text and become a good reader. Questions can be of the following types:

- *Global* questions are used to check whether the learners have understood the gist or central idea of the text. These questions are often set as pre-reading questions given to the learner before she/he reads a text, so that reading has a purpose.
- *Specific* questions are asked to get learners to locate details which are relevant to the development of the text. For example, one might need to know when Scott began his journey to the South Pole to understand its duration towards the end of the text.
- *Multiple-choice* questions can be simple or challenging. The variation in the level is controlled by the distractors supplied.
- *True/false* statements seem easy to make, but the teacher must be careful in using this type of question, for it often becomes a guessing game in the class. A good idea would be to follow up true/false questions with further questions like 'Why do you think so?' or 'Which part in the text gives you this information?'.
- *Open-ended* questions and statements generally ask for the learner's/reader's interpretation of the text. These are not difficult to set, but a teacher must be careful in handling the answer. She/he must not be autocratic but must encourage learners to put forward their views and ideas and to substantiate them.

Other techniques to teach reading

JUMBLED SENTENCES OR PARAGRAPHS

The different parts of a text are connected through cohesive (grammatical) devices and also through coherence (meaning). A small story/paragraph is divided into sentences and jumbled up. Learners have to put it in order. For example:

Reorder the sentences of the joke below so that it becomes meaningful.

'I've swallowed a marble', said the smaller boy.
Two boys turned up at a doctor's clinic.
'No', said the other boy, 'I own the marble.'
'I see', replied the doctor, 'and is this your brother?'

Arrange the jumbled sentences below in the right order.

Now scientists have developed a cream derived from the chilli's active ingredient, capsaicin.
The cream blocks pain signals from nerves just under the skin.
Chillies can burn the mouth and blister the skin.
But in South America, ground chillies have been used to help relieve pain for centuries.

Reference devices

A text is taken and reference devices underlined or circled. Learners have to say what they refer to.

When Columbus discovered Cuba in 1942, he also discovered tobacco! And it is the influence of this discovery that has had the greatest impact on the world.

Linking devices/linkers

The teacher presents a passage with the linkers deleted. The linkers are given in jumbled order in a box or as a list. Learners work out what the missing linkers are.

It was still winter, ... on Sunday the weather was fine. We decided to go on a trip to the seaside. The sun was bright .... warm, ... we did not go into the water. .... we walked along the shore .... looked at the ships. In the evening, we returned home. ...., a strong wind began to blow .... it began to rain. ...., we sat round a warm fire. We did not mind the weather at all.

then but and and but instead so and

Prediction

The teacher gives learners a part of a text or story, and asks them to predict what comes next. This task activates the schemata[4] in the learners' minds. Instead of a few lines of the story/text, the title can be given and learners asked to make predictions about what the text contains. For example:

Mouse trap   Food from the sea   Seven days to happy living

[4] Schemata/schema theory: Each of us has a structure for organising information held in memory. We use this schema to process new information. This is a source which can be tapped for teaching reading strategies.

DIFFERENT VERSIONS

Two or more versions of the same story or incident are given, and learners asked to read and interpret the writer's point of view. Newspaper editorials and reports or magazine articles on the same topic are sources which can be exploited in using this technique.

ESTIMATE, READ, RESPOND, AND QUESTION TECHNIQUE

The ERRQ strategy was developed by Dorothy Watson in 1985. The aim is to get the reader to link what she/he has with new information.

First, the learners estimate what the text will be like.	Skimming Scanning
Then they read the text through and respond to it.	Questions Tasks
Finally, they question things about the text itself or their response to the text.	What is the author actually trying to say? Do I accept what she/he says? Why were these portions of the text difficult?

LITERARY SOCIOGRAMS

Developed by Johnson and Louis (1985), this technique depicts the characters in the story and their interrelationship. This technique, used generally with literary texts, helps the reader to get a better insight into the text. For example:

Old Man and the Sea

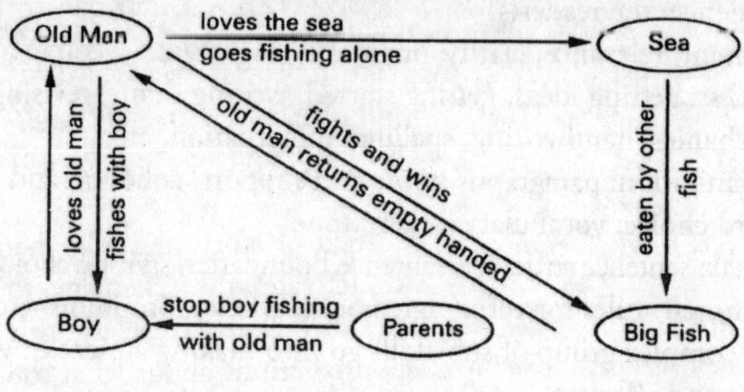

THINK IT OVER

1. Can some of the techniques outlined above be used to teach writing skills?

2. Which techniques would you use to teach reading in class 7?
3. How did you learn to read in your mother tongue? Did you start with alphabets and words, and then go on to texts? When did you learn to read signboards?

Application

Take a prescribed textbook and see how many techniques to teach reading skills are used in the exercise types.

Mastery of vocabulary and an understanding of how English grammar operates are desirable if one has to become a good reader. These two aspects will be dealt with in detail in later sections.

Writing

Writing is perhaps one of the most demanding of skills. It has to be deliberately cultivated. Unlike listening and speaking, it is not something which is natural to humans—it is a skill which has been developed in civilised society to pass on knowledge or messages beyond the constraints of the here and now.

All writing aims at clear and efficient communication. But what goes into clear and efficient communication? Raimes (1983) lists the factors that one must consider when producing a piece of writing that is clear, fluent, and capable of communicating ideas effectively:

- Purpose: the reason for writing
- Audience: the reader(s)
- Content: relevance, clarity, originality, logic, etc.
- Process: getting ideas, getting started, writing drafts, revising
- Mechanics: handwriting, spelling, punctuation, etc.
- Organisation: paragraphs, topic and support, cohesion and unity
- Word choice: vocabulary, idiom, tone
- Syntax: sentence structure, sentence boundaries, stylistic choices, etc.
- Grammar: rules for verbs, agreement, articles, pronouns, etc.

Thus, a complex group of sub-skills go into making a piece of writing coherent and effective.

In writing, even a simple thing like the direction of writing can be a problem. In English, we write from left to write, but learners whose primary schooling has been in Urdu or Japanese will have learnt to write from right to left or top to bottom.

THINK IT OVER

1. Re-read Raimes's list (above). In which areas do you think your learners need most help?
2. In which areas would you need to employ different techniques?

In this section, we will take up different sub-skills of writing and discuss possible techniques. These techniques can be used in different classes, depending on when students begin to learn English. (For example, in Tamil Nadu, English begins in class 3, and in Karnataka, in class 5.)

Mechanics of writing

Writing begins very often at the pre-primary level when learners are asked to copy or trace out letters. Some of the techniques used to teach the mechanics of writing are given below.

COPYING EXERCISES

This begins early and continues for quite a few years. There are different kinds of copying exercises.

Copying sentences from texts

This technique gives learners confidence as copying work will be almost error-free. A variation of this technique is to give a list of items and ask learners to copy them in the relevant column. For example:

bus	jug	bed	table
car	tram	plate	cup
chair	saucer	train	stool

transport	crockery	furniture

Matching words/pictures to copied-out sentences

Learners are asked to copy out sentences and put them in the right place next to a matching word or image. For example:

I had to stop at a railway crossing on the way to school.

The wiring is old. It has to be changed.

The tap needs a new washer.

plumber ....

bus driver ....

electrician ....

Identifying and copying out correct sentences

Correct and incorrect sentences are given. Learners are asked to copy out the correct ones. For example:

Billo go to school every day.
Ramu loves gulab jamuns.
Asma studies hard.
Did Billo went to school on Sunday?
No, Asma and Ramu did go.
They made preparations for the Independence Day celebrations.

Copying out sentences according to theme

A set of sentences is given, and learners copy out and arrange them according to their themes. For example:

Mangoes are grown almost all over India.
Some insects have wings and others do not.
The housefly, mosquito, honey-bee and cockroach are examples of insects that have wings.
They vary in colour. Some are red and others a golden yellow.
Their taste and flavour too vary.
Mangoes are the favourite fruit of many people.
They were enjoyed by kings like Akbar and Shahjahan.
However, they cannot be called birds.

mangoes	insects

Substitution tables

This too is a copying technique. Substitution tables can be simple or complex. For example:

(a) I like

I like	dancing.
	swimming.
	reading.
	riding.

(b)

After finishing my	homework,	I went to	school.
	dinner,		bed.
	exercises,		the market.

(c)

Saba went to buy a present for her	younger sister.
	cousin.
	baby brother.

'The	dolls	on the top shelf	look very nice',
	aeroplanes	in the window	
	teddy bears	in the case	

she said to the shopkeeper. 'What kind of	doll
	aeroplane
	teddy bear

do you want?' asked the shopkeeper. 'I have	dolls that walk.'
	aeroplanes that fly.'
	teddy bears that cry.'

'I want one that	you can make yourself',	said Megha.
	is soft',	
	you can dress and undress',	

'Oh, I don't have those', said the shopkeeper. 'Won't these do?'

Think it over

1. Is there any difference between the types of copying techniques listed above? Are they all the same?
2. Which copying exercises would you use in class 7?

Spelling and punctuation

Identifying correctly spelt words

A list of words is given, and the correctly spelt words have to be identified.

Blank-filling activities

Here, certain areas which pose spelling problems can be identified, and learners asked to fill in the blanks. For example:

ie or ei?	rec __ __ ve	c __ __ ling	dec __ __ ve
	h __ __ fer	b __ __ ge	
ea or ee?	pl __ __ se	ch __ __ t	sh __ __ t
	tr __ __ t	str __ __ t	qu __ __ n

Jumbled words

Letters of a word are given in jumbled order, and learners are asked to put them in order. Words which usually pose a problem (especially long words) can be used for this activity. For example:

vienmenront *(environment)* cendsed *(descend)*
timmoc *(commit)* denpretis *(president)*
geualang *(language)* otpeosaphr *(apostrophe)*

This can be played as a game in class.

Capitals and stops

At an early stage, single sentences can be given and learners asked to supply the punctuation marks. For example:

sita ate an apple today
our school is closed on sunday

Later, more than one sentence or a short paragraph can be given with the number of punctuation marks required. For example:

the children went to bed early they had to leave for delhi the next day *(three capital letters and two full stops)*

why didnt you ask the teacher about this asked rupa *(two capital letters, one apostrophe, one pair of inverted commas, one question mark and one full stop)*

At a more advanced level, complete units of discourse can be given, and learners asked to insert all the punctuation marks required, and to divide the text into paragraphs. For example:

a man ordered a large pizza do you want me to cut it into six pieces or eight asked the waiter better make it six i don't think i can eat eight pieces the man said

Spaces

A sentence without spaces can be given, and learners asked to rewrite it with correct spacing. For example:

Fromtheverybeginningmilkhasbeentreatedastheperfectfood

(From the very beginning, milk has been treated as the perfect food.)

Apostrophes

Learners often have problems in deciding where to use the apostrophe. A technique which can be used for this is to give paraphrases and to ask learners to give the required version, with apostrophes, or give the learners the genitive possessive forms with apostrophes and ask them to give the paraphrased versions. For example:

the books belonging to the boys	the boys' books
the car owned by the man	the man's car
the parents of the girls	the girls' parents

or

a week's holiday	a holiday for a week
a minute's rest	rest for a minute
a rupee's rice	rice for a rupee

SYNTAX

Techniques under this head should lead learners to understand how words combine to form sentences, and the rules which govern this. (Techniques for grammar and vocabulary will be dealt with in detail in separate sections.)

Blank filling

This can include discrete sentences or paragraphs. The blanks could be grammar items, cohesive devices or content words (vocabulary). For example:

(a) Verb forms

> Dear Soha,
> We are enjoying our holiday in Ooty very much. We .... (go) for long walks every day. The scenery .... (be) marvellous. Yesterday, I .... (ride) a pony! Tomorrow, we .... (visit) Emerald Lake. I .... (wish) you .... (be) here.
> Love,
> Darshan

(b) Cohesive devices

The cat joined the Re-education Committee and was very active in .... for some days. She was seen one day sitting on a roof and talking to some sparrows who were just out of .... reach. .... was telling .... that all animals were now comrades ...

Orwell 1945

(c) Collocations

I want a cup of .... coffee. (strong, powerful)
She was told to abstain .... (without, from) alcohol.
Writing paper will be supplied free of .... (charge, price).
He is a .... (continuous, chain) smoker. He smokes up to fifty cigarettes a day.

Completion

Learners are asked to complete sentences and dialogues. For example:

(a) Sentences

I would have acted differently ....
Look! There is the man ....
My teacher rarely ....
Can you tell me how ....

(b) Dialogue

A Hello!
B ....! ....?
A ....?
B To the exhibition. Do you want to come?
A ....?
B Haven't you heard about the one being organised by Disney?
A No. ....?
B Of course it'll be fun! You can meet Mickey and Donald.

Identifying styles

Here, sentences or short texts are given, and the learner is asked to identify who might say or write them. For example:

(a) Sentences

Smile, please.
Read the second last line on the chart, please.
It's a boy, Mr Arora. Congratulations!
Plain naan or butter naan?

(b) Texts

Feeding a dog naturally varies according to the breed. As a general rule, however, every dog should have one good meal a day.

Bhanupriya is popular all over the country. What is it that makes her the favourite of everyone in the film world? I think I have discovered the secret of her popularity.

Ladies and gentlemen, it gives me great pleasure to introduce to you the king of ghazals. A big hand, please, for Aziz Mian!

This is with reference to your letter dated 10 October 2020. I regret to inform you that …

A variation of this is to give learners a situation with many utterances and ask them to make a stylistic choice.

Organisation

PARAGRAPHS

A paragraph should have a clear, controlling idea (topic sentence), good supporting sentences, and a definite conclusion.

Identification

Using this technique, learners can be made aware of the organisational aspects as well as the content of a paragraph. Two example activities are given below.

Activity 1: Look at the paragraphs below. Which paragraph has a clear controlling idea? Which paragraph is well developed?

a. I love boating on the lake near my home. My home is in Ooty, Tamil Nadu. Tamil Nadu is a very progressive state. Recently, many new industries have been started in this state.

b. Mr Kanjoos is the meanest man I have ever known. Everything about him lacks generosity. His eyes are small, his lips are thin, and his voice is cold and unfriendly. He is very rich, yet he wears shabby clothes. He never buys fresh fruits or vegetables. He has never given a rupee as donation. He is the type to give a beggar fifty paise and ask for change.

Activity 2: Read the paragraph below. You will find that some sentences do not properly belong to it. Underline the sentences.

The two brothers were quite different. Bob was tall, fair and slim; John was short, dark and fat. Bob was like his mother, and John was like his father. Bob was never happier than when he had something practical to do; John, on the other hand, was clumsy when using his hands. Their sister, Mary, was also clumsy with her hands. Bob rarely spoke to other people unless he was spoken to first, but John was always the centre of a group, talking and chattering away as if his life depended on it. I am sure you have friends like this. In fact, they were so different that it was hard to believe they were brothers.

Chaplen 1970

Making outlines and notes

This technique requires learners to give the outline of a paragraph in the form of notes. A sample paragraph may be as follows:

Pluto is the god of the underworld. Rocks formed in the deeper layers of the earth are thus named 'plutonic'. There are a number of plutonic rocks. Granite and gabbro are two common varieties among them.

Notes for the above paragraph could be arranged linearly:

Topic: Plutonic rock
Support: – Where formed
– Types: granite, gabbro

The outline can also be in the form of branching notes.

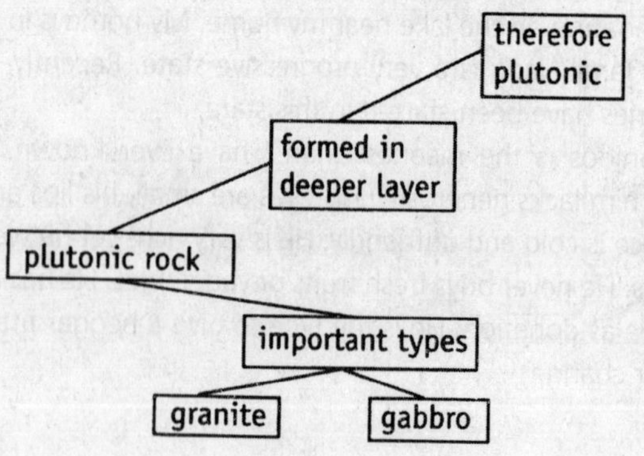

A well-written and organised text should be chosen for note making. Literary texts, where there is a movement back and forth in time, should be avoided while teaching this skill. At a later stage, learners could be asked to tackle complex texts.

Production

There are different techniques of enabling the production of a paragraph.

EXPANSION OF STRUCTURE

Points are given and learners asked to develop paragraphs. It is a very good technique to use in the early stages of written production, as it helps learners to write coherently. Two example activities are shown below.

(a) Giving an opening sentence

It was an extremely untidy room that I entered. *(Continue, using the points below.)*

- bed not made
- orange peels and pips on floor
- room not dusted
- books and clothes scattered all over
- cupboard stuffed with clothes

(b) Using diagrams

Instructions for filtering and boiling water

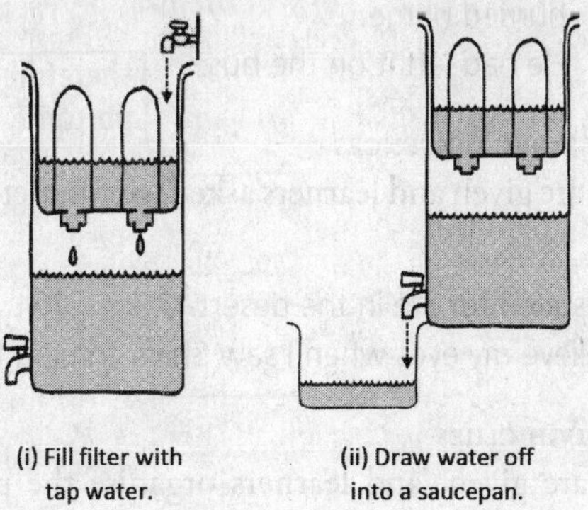

(i) Fill filter with tap water.

(ii) Draw water off into a saucepan.

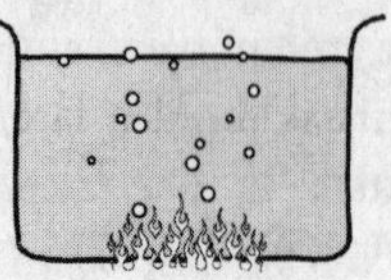

(iii) Heat water.
Let it boil for five minutes.

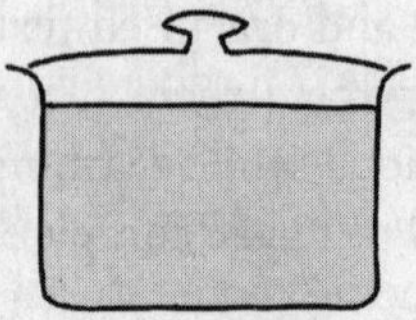

(iv) Cover pan with a lid.
Leave water to cool.

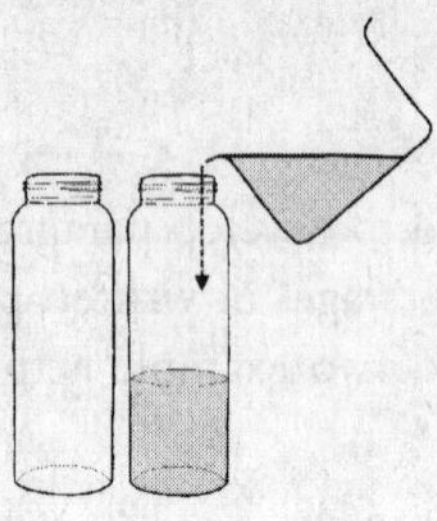

(v) When cool, pour water
into clean bottles.

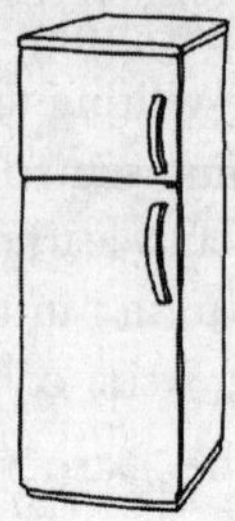

(vi) Store bottles
in refrigerator.

EXPANSION USING BEGINNING AND ENDING

First and last sentences are given, and learners asked to develop a paragraph based on these. For example:

First sentence: We were shown into a long, low room.
Last sentence: I do not expect to see a more beautiful room ever again.
First sentence: Bhagat jumped off the bus before it stopped, and hurried home.
Last sentence: He had left it on the bus.

EXPANSION FROM TOPIC SENTENCES

Topic sentences are given and learners asked to complete the paragraph. For example:

Camels are well-suited for life in the desert.
I could hardly believe my eyes when I saw Shiva coming towards me.

EXPANSION THROUGH CLUES

Sentence clues are given, and learners organise the paragraph using these clues in a syntactically and semantically acceptable manner. For example:

a hundred years ago / less specialisation / than today. / furniture maker / made / full table. / furniture he made / very good / and beautiful / but / take him / long time / make it. / modern furniture / made in factories. / man / working / furniture factory / one process / for example, making legs. / division of labour / more furniture made / affordable prices. / will quality suffer / is the question.

Also refer to re-ordering jumbled sentences into a coherent paragraph in the section on techniques of reading (page 131). This technique can be used as a pre-writing task, especially if the paragraphs have linking devices connecting sentences.

The writing process

The writing process can begin with brainstorming sessions to get ideas. If the learner has no ideas, there will be nothing to communicate.

Another important aspect of the writing process involves finding out through discussions or through critiquing sessions whether the ideas are relevant, original, clear, logical, and whether anybody would want to read what is written.

This leads to the question of the purpose of writing as well as the audience. Thus, it would be meaningless to ask a learner to write a letter to his/her sister inviting her to a birthday party when both live in the same house. Similarly, if learners were to write to an insurance company about the damage to their car in an accident, the manner of writing would be totally different from what they would use if they were to write to a friend about the same accident.

A rough draft is written first and then revised. Writing drafts is a good practice as many slips and errors get edited out in this process.

Let us now consider some other techniques which are used to teach the process of writing. These techniques make use of various kinds of input.

Using pictures

These can be used as input to write either descriptive or narrative pieces. Many examinations such as the ICSE and the CBSE make use of picture input in their question papers. In textbooks, writing tasks which use pictures are called guided composition.

Using maps

Maps are used to set tasks on giving directions or describing physical features. A map can also be used to describe the country through which a journey takes place.

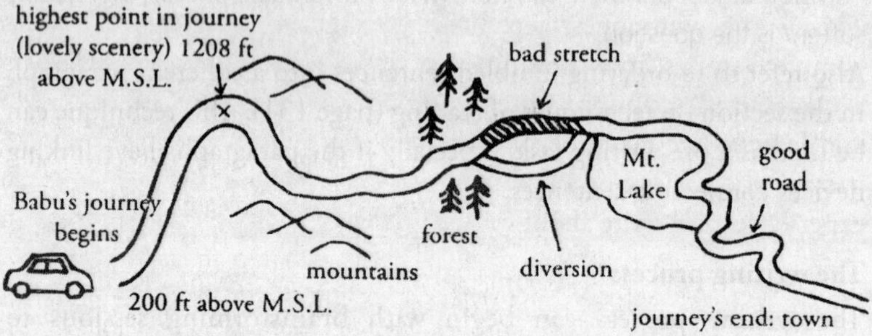

Describe Babu's journey in your own words.

Using diagrams, figures, charts, tables

These forms of input are used to transfer information contained in them into continuous discourse.

Xanadu's budget for 2022–2023

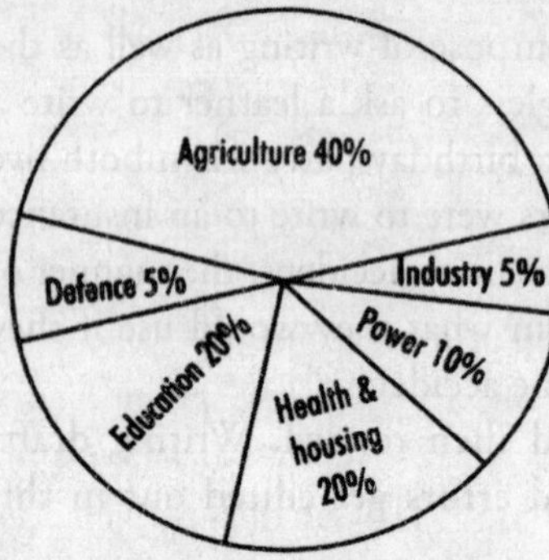

Write a short paragraph on the 2022–2023 budget of the small kingdom of Xanadu.

Total income: 3 million tokens

Other than pie charts, bar graphs, graphs and tables can also be used. For example, learners could be asked to use the information in the table below to write a brief paragraph comparing three makes of cars.

MAKE	COST	MILEAGE	MAINTENANCE
Maruti 1000	Rs 3.8 lakh	15 km/l	difficult; spare parts in special shops
Ambassador	Rs 4.7 lakh	13 km/l	easy; can improvise
Fiat NE 118	Rs 5.9 lakh	16 km/l	not very difficult; can manage

Family trees can also be used to get learners to do a piece of continuous writing.[5] A biodata or curriculum vitae too can be used as input for a writing task that is generally descriptive.

USING PASSAGES AND EXTRACTS

This is the commonest technique used to help learners write or complete stories, to write from a different point of view, or to write a character description. Often passages and extracts act as stimuli, and learners are taken beyond the text. For example, learners read a passage about a fire or a fair and are asked to relate this to their own experiences and write about it.

THINK IT OVER

Can you think of two activities, other than those given above, which can be used to teach writing? At what level would you use them?

APPLICATION

No specific mention has been made of letter writing in this section. In groups, choose three techniques from those given in the chapter which can be used to do letter writing.

INTEGRATING SKILLS

> The integration of skills in the language classroom can be defined quite simply as a series of activities or tasks which use any combination of the four skills—Listening (L), Speaking (S), Reading (R), Writing (W)—in a continuous and related sequence.
>
> Read 1985

Let us now consider some techniques which make learners use more than one skill.

LISTENING AND NOTE MAKING

Here learners listen to an audio or to the teacher and make notes. The note making can be guided in the early stages and become more free in the later stages. For example:

---

[5] Refer to the use of family trees in the section on 'Listening', p. 109.

Listen to the audio and makes notes on points 1 and 2. Listen again and make notes on points 3–6.

Fred Gipson, author of several books about Texas, was born in 1908. He grew up on a farm and, from an early age, took on every job from cotton picking to driving a tractor. He studied at the University of Texas, and later worked as a newspaper reporter and feature writer.
In 1940, he married, and then decided to try his luck as a freelance writer. Before achieving success in famous magazines, he wrote outdoor and adventure stories which were widely published. Gipson is best known for his novels *Hound-Dog Man* and *Old Yeller*.
He now lives with his wife and two sons in his old family home, where he writes and manages a small livestock farm.

Notes

1. Gipson's year of birth
2. Year he got married
3. Jobs he has done
4. Books he has written
5. Present occupation
6. Family details

From the notes made, learners can be asked to write a short passage on the author.

Dictation

This technique acts as a bridge between the spoken and the written form. It integrates the skills of listening and writing. The sub-skills under listening include understanding the content and identifying weak forms, contracted forms and pauses. The sub-skills of writing include punctuation and spelling.

Drama

This technique includes all four skills in varying degrees at different levels. At an elementary level it can be a reading–speaking–listening activity. Later it can involve writing–conversation–listening–reading–speaking.

Information-gap activity

This involves transfer of given information from one person to another—or from one form to another, or from one place to another—generally calling for the decoding or encoding of information from or into language. One example is pair work in

> which each member of a pair has a part of the total information (for example, an incomplete picture) and attempts to convey it verbally to the other.
>
> Prabhu 1987

Information-gap activities can be done using written input; learners are given different clues from which they have to find out who did something or where something is. These activities can be done in small groups or pairs too. For example, two versions of a map are given, and in pairs learners have to complete their versions by asking and answering questions. (Note that the maps shown below are for advanced learners. One can devise maps in which the task is much easier.)

Learner A's map **(learner A is at Camp X)**

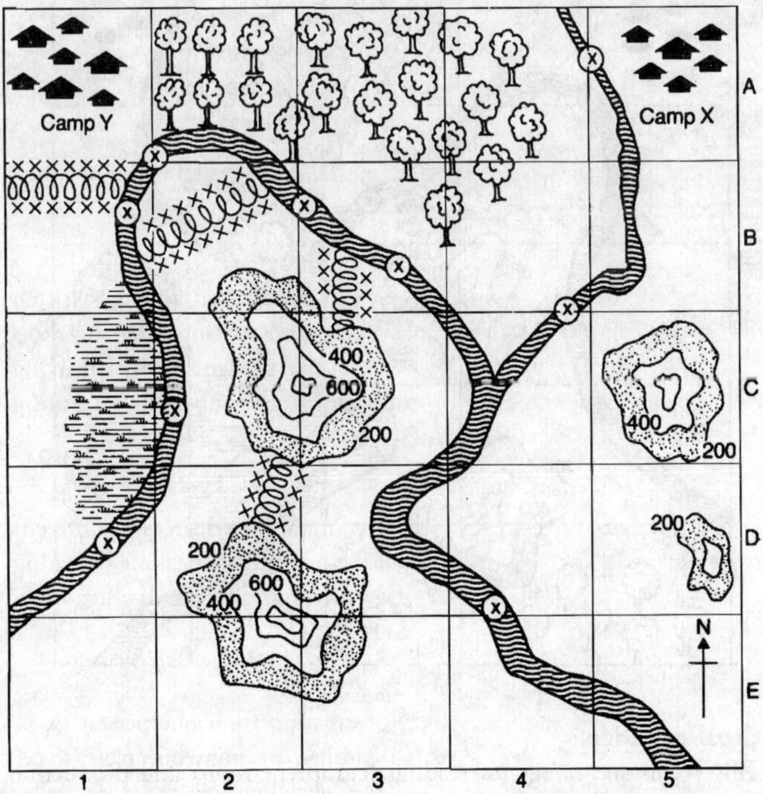

This key to the symbols used in the maps is given to both learners

= *Forest.* Do not enter this area. It is mined and contains dangerous animals.

= *Swamp* Do not cross this area. It is impassable to men and vehicles.

= *Hill.* Do not cross this area. It is heavily guarded by the enemy.

= *Barbed Wire Barricades and Electric Fences.* Avoid these obstacles.

= *Ford.* The rivers may be crossed by men and vehicles *only* at these places.

Learner B's map (learner B is at Camp Y)

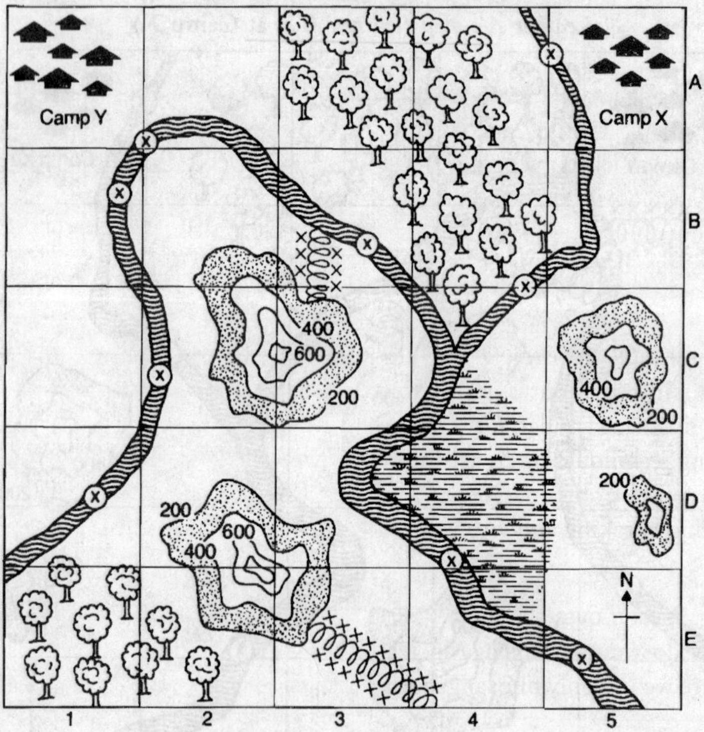

CLOZE DIALOGUE

This technique integrates reading (comprehension) and production (writing). After completing the dialogue, learners do role play. For example:

A Hello!
B ....
A ....
B I'd like to go watch a film today.
A ....
B 'Jurassic Park'.
A What time does it start?
B ....
A Why don't you look up the papers?
B I will. Do you want to come with me?
A Yes; if I can get some money.
B ....
A No; she gave me some yesterday.
B Can't you ask your father?
A No; I don't think I can.
B ....
A I spilt ink on his office papers.
B ....
A I was filling my pen.
B Oh dear! You won't be able to come with me.
A ....
B Yes. Bye.
A ....

Information transfer

Here, information is transferred from one mode to the other—linguistic to tabular, or tabular to linguistic. Listening and note taking techniques often use information transfer. Information may be transferred from a passage to a table and vice versa, or from maps to writing/speaking and vice versa.

Think it over

How do we use language in real life? Can you think of a situation where we use only one language skill?

Section summary

- Language involves four main skills—listening, speaking, reading, and writing.

- Each skill has many sub-skills.
- Learning the skills of a language can be divided broadly into skill-getting and skill-using.
- Different techniques are listed with examples under two broad heads: listening and speaking, and reading and writing.
- There are some techniques which require learners to use more than one skill. Such techniques integrate two or more skills.

Did you understand?

1. What is the difference between approach, method and technique?
2. Why should a teacher have more than one technique at his/her command?
3. What do skill-getting techniques help learners to master?
4. How are these different from skill-using activities?
5. What language skills come naturally to us? Which language skills do we have to learn?

Application

Task 1

Given below are some techniques. Think of activities using these. Name the skills they expect learners to use.

Technique	Activities	Skills
drills		
dialogues		
riddles and games		
dictation		

Task 2

Given below are a few activity types outlined in this chapter. How can you expand them to make learners use more language skills in an integrated manner?

a. flow charts ('Listening', p. 110)
b. rhymes ('Speaking', p. 114)
c. dictionary work ('Reading', p. 129)
d. using pictures ('Writing', p. 145)

TASK 3

a. Given below are two activity inputs (visuals), but the activities have not been described. How would you exploit these inputs? What skills would learners be using? At what level would you use them?

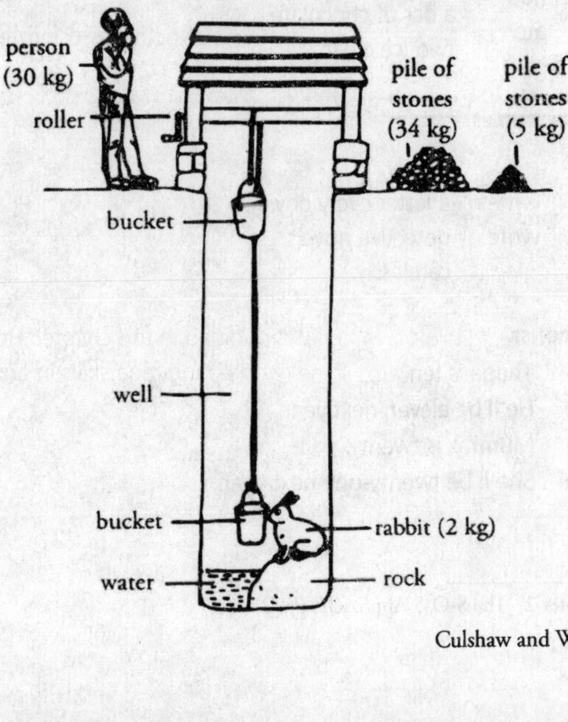

Culshaw and Waters 1984

b. Prepare a lesson plan for the activity in each case, detailing the following: (i) level of learners, (ii) skills demanded by task/activity, (iii) skill-getting/skill-using.

TECHNIQUES OF TEACHING GRAMMAR

The techniques of teaching grammar depend on certain key areas of focus. These areas may be identified with reference to the practice and use of grammar.

Practice	Use
drill	
contextualised clues	communicative
communicative	

Practice: Drill

Drills can be of the following types.[6]

Substitution tables

He She Raja Rani	had ate	an apple. a bar of chocolate. two ice creams.

Structure tables

He I They You She	writes write	clearly. a letter every day. detective novels. carelessly.

Cue–response

Teacher	Thapa is ten.
Response	He'll be eleven next year.
Teacher	Mumtaz is twenty.
Response	She'll be twenty-one next year.

[6] See Chapter 2, 'The S-O-S Approach', pp. 27–30.

Teacher   Baby likes banana.
Response   Baby doesn't like banana.
Teacher   I like tennis.
Response   I don't like tennis.

Practice: Contextualised clues

In this type of exercise, the context provides the clue to the type of grammatical item to be used. Here are three ways in which this could be done.

TECHNIQUE 1

Follow the example below and respond to the given situations.

SITUATION (CUE): The telephone's ringing.

RESPONSE: I'll answer it.

a. The washing is outside, and it starts to rain.
b. Your father cannot understand a letter written in Odia.
c. Your friend says he is thirsty.

TECHNIQUE 2

Respond to the given situations.

a. A friend has come to see you in your house. Offer him something to drink.
b. You are in a post office. You need three stamps for a letter to the USA. What do you say?

TECHNIQUE 3

Complete the following letter using verbs in either the simple present or the present progressive.

Dear Bhavna,

We .... (enjoy) our holiday a lot. Every day we .... (walk) down to the beach, ... (take) a dip in the sea, ... (go) for a ride, and .... (have) lunch at Tropicana. In fact, I .... (write) this letter from Tropicana. We .... (wish) you were here. I .... (hope) your internship .... (go) well.

Love,

Lata

Practice: Communicative

Here, the grammar to be practised is based on information-gap or opinion-gap activities. The general framework is given, but the language is not controlled strictly.

Communicative question-asking activity

Through twenty 'yes/no' questions, learners try to discover the person, animal or thing the teacher has thought of. Later, a learner can take the role of the teacher. For example:

Learner 1 Are you alive?
Teacher No.
Learner 2 Did you really exist?
Teacher Yes.
Learner 3 Were you a man?
Teacher Yes.
Learner 4 Were you Indian?
Teacher No.
(... and so on till completion)

Story completion

The first line of a story is given, and learners are asked to build on it. For example:

Last night I got locked out of my house because ...

Shipwrecked

This is a popular communicative activity and it is included in many modern grammar texts. The language is not controlled strictly, but the type of activity dictates to a great extent the type of language to be used. An example of this type of activity is given below.

You are one of the five surviving crew members of a small ship that sank off the coast of a large desert island. You and your companions must walk 100 kilometres to the opposite side of the island where other ships are likely to pass. You can survive only if you reach the other side of the island.

Choose the seven most critical items for the 100-kilometre trip from the things that have been saved from the ship. You cannot take everything as you are weak and have to walk a long way. Work in groups of five. You must defend each of your choices with a good reason.

a box of matches	40 litres of water in 14-kilogram cans
50 feet of nylon rope	a first aid kit
a portable stove	two signal flares
a flashlight with batteries	two pistols
a magnetic compass	a tin of powdered milk
a world map	a life raft
some tinned food	a copy of the Koran
a copy of the Bible	a solar-powered FM radio
a receiver-transmitter	

You will notice that learners will tend to use the structure 'If we take … then …' or the conjunction 'because'.[7]

PROBLEM SOLVING

Simple to complex problems can be given as input, and again, certain grammatical items will be used with greater frequency than others during the course of the activity.

A farmer, who had a young goat, cut a huge bundle of grass and wanted to take both of them to the town across the river to sell. He had also captured a tiger, which he wanted to give to a zoo. The river could be crossed only by using a small boat. This boat could carry only the weight of two persons or animals or items at a time. How did the farmer manage to cross the river?

Use: Communicative

At this level, learners are given activities based on different skills. The learner uses the language/grammar that is required to do the task. Here the approach is holistic.

LISTENING AND RESPONDING

Listening and doing

- Listening and drawing
- Listening and locating

---

[7] You may have noticed that grammar practice through communicative activities does not focus on one grammatical item to the exclusion of others, but on a variety of items that can be used to convey the message.

- Listening and speaking (communicative activities with different sets of cards or pictures)
- Dictation[8]

Dictogloss

This is an activity for advanced-level learners. A passage is read three times. Learners listen to the passage for the meaning, and are allowed to jot down only what they consider key words. They then reproduce the passage. Here the learners *use* the language to complete the task. The passage being read out can be selected or prepared by the teacher such that it contains many examples of the grammatical structures being studied. A sample passage is given below.

The Arctic and Antarctic are very cold. Snow falling there has very little chance of melting. There are large stretches of snow compacted into ice, called 'glaciers', covering land and sea. Similarly, on high mountains there are thick sheets of ice covering the slopes and filling the valleys.

SPEAKING AND DOING

- Giving directions (learner–learner activity)
- Producing dialogues
- Role play (controlled/free)
- Producing skits/drama

READING AND WRITING

- Passages: blank filling, completion
- Graphs: explaining, drawing inferences
- Timetables: school, railway
- Texts
    - completion
    - manipulation and completion
    - elicitation

[8] When dictation is given at normal speed, learners have to identify the structures used (along with the characteristics of the spoken form of language) in order to write. This very often includes the learner's use of his/her knowledge of language structures to do the task.

APPLICATION

TASK 1

For the activities listed under the 'Use: Communicative' section, decide what grammatical item can be the focus of the activity. For example, the use of the imperative form is the focus of the 'listening and doing' activity below.

Stand up; go to the table.
Pick up the red pencil; come back to your place.
Sit down.

TASK 2

Write out a complete task for one of the following activities, and name the grammatical item that forms its focus.

a. Listening and speaking
b. Role play
c. Timetable

If you look at the different types of exercises from drills to communicative exercises, you will notice two things.

- The rubrics or introduction to the task becomes increasingly elaborate, beginning with a line such as 'Make as many sentences as possible in a substitution table' to instructions that later extend to almost a paragraph. This is because grammar techniques move away from sentence generation to discourse generation.
- The exercises which are communicative in nature do not deal with one item of grammar (for example, Type 1 of the *if* clause). They subsume a broader area of language (say, conditionals for problem solving). This means that learners make use of whatever conditional clause is required or appropriate to do the task.

In this chapter, there is necessarily an overlap among different techniques, especially with those which are communicative in nature. This illustrates the point that the communicative approach deals with language holistically and not discretely.

TECHNIQUES OF TEACHING VOCABULARY

Vocabulary teaching and learning begins from the first day of school and continues throughout one's academic career. We learn vocabulary whenever we come into contact with a new language and try to use it. We are considered 'good' users of language when we are capable of using words effectively.

In this section, we will consider vocabulary-teaching techniques in terms of their use in the classroom and the task types that match these techniques.

Techniques for classroom use

Realia/objects

Objects in the classroom or those brought from outside can be used to teach vocabulary. This way of teaching vocabulary is especially effective at the primary level. Objects that can be used include, for example, 'bag', 'pencil', 'chalk', 'table', 'lunchbox', 'leaf', 'pebble', 'seed', 'flower' and 'key'.

Pictures

Another effective way of getting learners to learn words is through the use of pictures. In the initial stages, pictures can be used for learning vocabulary orally. Later, learners can be asked to match words with pictures. This technique is again very effective at the primary level. At a later stage, colourful pictures from magazines or Sunday newspapers can be used as input for teaching vocabulary. For example, words related to a bicycle, such as 'handlebars', 'chain', 'wheel', 'spokes', 'fork', etc., can be taught using a picture of a bicycle. Later, the same picture can serve as input for further work, for example, in writing a description of a bicycle.

Texts

Texts are often the only resource a teacher has for teaching vocabulary. There are some interesting techniques for teaching vocabulary in an innovative way using texts in the class.

Technique 1

Select words in the text which you want the learners to learn. Give the meanings of these in a mixed-up order on the blackboard. Ask the class to go through the text and find the words that fit the meanings.

If you have a small class and facilities to photocopy, you could try a different method. Replace certain words in a text with their synonyms or with paraphrases. Put the original words on the blackboard or prepare card sets. Working in groups or pairs, the class puts the original words back in the text. Look at the example below.

One day a jackal was wandering about the forest in search of food. Suddenly from somewhere nearby he heard an odd noise. He was held by fear, for he thought it was an enemy who had come to attack him. At first he thought of running away; then, he made up his mind to discover what it was.

FIND OUT | UNUSUAL | ROAMING | GRIPPED | DECIDED

Technique 2

A second technique is to supply a text with nonsense words to the class and write a list of words on the blackboard. Ask the class to replace the nonsense words with appropriate words from the list.

Bimal and his bittoni sister Tara lived with their tholer and father on the hillside of a tithful valley. Their father was a romder and the family lived in a little vamfous. The vamfous clung to the steep hillside above a small hallit at the stoman of the valley.

FARMER | LITTLE | FARMHOUSE | BEAUTIFUL | MOTHER | VILLAGE | BOTTOM

Technique 3

Another way of using this technique is to use words from another language in the text instead of nonsense words. In case learners know the other language being used, a list of English words need not be given; for example, using Hindi in the text (as shown below) for learners familiar with Hindi.

Magarmach look like bada lizards. Although their maximum lambayi can be as much as tees feet, most of them are much smaller than this. They live in nadiyaan and swamps, feeding on the unwary janwar that come there to drink.

These types of text exploitation for vocabulary teaching are useful at the primary level.

CONTEXT

Vocabulary teaching becomes meaningful when it is done in context. A word gets its meaning from its context. This awareness can be brought about by doing tasks based on dictionary work, which will help learners learn and consolidate commonly used words, phrases, idioms and proverbs. A set of sentences is given, and learners try to find the exact meaning of the underlined words using a dictionary.

The chosen items could be of different kinds, as in the examples below.

Content words

The bank charges are 10%.
Who is in charge here?
The police arrested him on the charge of murder.
The battery is fully charged.

Verbs and phrasal verbs

The actress was heavily made up.
The accountant was asked to make up the difference in amount.
I am making up a parcel of old clothes for the jumble sale.
That little girl is forever making up stories.

Plural forms with special meanings

Just a minute!
Have you typed the minutes of the last meeting?

Is it made of glass?
I can't see a thing without my glasses.

Idioms and proverbs

IDIOMS
to burn the candle at both ....
to .... the beans
to bark up the wrong ....

PROVERBS
More ...., less speed.
No news is good ....
A bird in .... is worth two in the bush.

VOCABULARY GAMES AND CROSSWORDS

These are useful for vocabulary expansion. Learners will have to think of all the words they know and try to complete the tasks. If they do not know the words, they can guess and then check their answers. Examples of some kinds of games are given below.

Before/after

EXAMPLE 1: Find a single prefix for the given letters so that a meaningful word is made. Afterwards, check your answers in a dictionary.

……cern	……vert	……dense	……cede
……fer	……found	……cur	……vict

EXAMPLE 2: Complete the following words. Their meanings have been given to help you. The number of blanks denotes the number of letters.

kn __ __ __	We cut with this
kn __ __ __	A playing card
kn __ __ __	We do this when we pray or beg
kn __ __ __	We do this to dough

Word ladders

EXAMPLE 1: With the help of the given clues, change COLD to HEAT by changing only one letter at a time.

C	O	L	D	
				to bend into two or more
				what you eat
				to cross a river on foot
				a place built for defence
				a town with a harbour
				gay; full of life
				fuel cut from a bog
H	E	A	T	

Answer: cold → fold → food → ford → fort → port → pert → peat → heat

EXAMPLE 2: With the help of the clues given, change ARM to LEG by changing only one letter at a time.

A	R	M	
			not bright
			large
L	E	G	

Answer: arm → aim → dim → dig → big → beg → leg

EXAMPLE 3: No clues given—change FISH to MEAT.

F	I	S	H
M	E	A	T

Answer: fish → fist → list → lest → nest → neat → meat

Word squares

Example 1: The letters which have to go into each square are given jumbled up. The learners solve it in such a way that meaningful words are made both horizontally and vertically.

	1	2	3	4
1	A	Y	S	E
2	H	E	A	C
3	W	H	O	S
4	S	W	E	Y

Answer

E	A	S	Y
A	C	H	E
S	H	O	W
Y	E	W	S

Example 2: Clues can be given instead of the letters of the word.

	1	2	3	4
1				
2				
3				
4				

Clues
1. A sound sent back
2. A fellow
3. A long-eared rodent
4. Not shut

Answer

E	C	H	O
C	H	A	P
H	A	R	E
O	P	E	N

Glidograms

A grid can be prepared and put either on the blackboard or on sheets of paper. The class is divided into groups and asked to solve the puzzle. The clues could be in the form of pictures (for primary- and middle-school children) or in the form of verbal hints (for high-school learners), as in the examples below.

T				
	T			
		T		
			T	
				T
			T	
		T		
	T			
T				

Picture clues

Verbal clues
1. Portable battery-powered hand light
2. Seen in the night sky
3. Used to fasten a door or gate
4. Half of a hundred
5. Opposite of last
6. Twice twenty

Answers

T	O	R	C	H
S	T	A	R	S
L	A	T	C	H
F	I	F	T	Y
F	I	R	S	T
F	O	R	T	Y

7. Used to light a stove or candle
8. Stuck on an envelope sent by post
9. Main stem of a tree

M	A	T	C	H
S	T	A	M	P
T	R	U	N	K

Crossword puzzles

Crosswords need time to be solved. They also need thinking. Ideally, they can be given as pair or group work in class, with enough time for learners to solve it. Crosswords can vary from the very simple to the very complex. At the primary level, simple crosswords can be given.

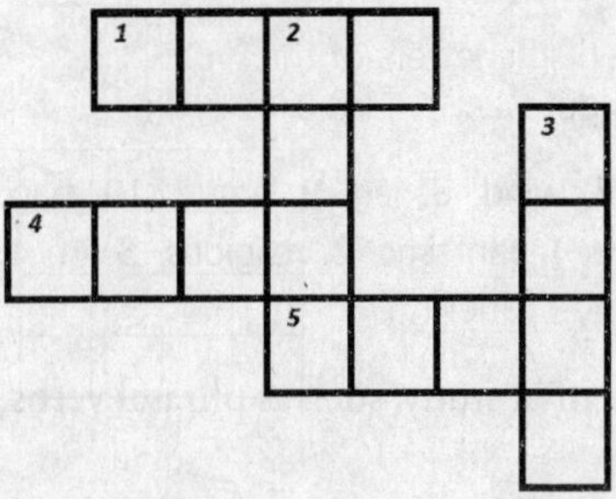

ACROSS

1. Mary had a little ....
4. Hot cross ....
5. Twinkle, twinkle, little ....

DOWN

2. Little .... Muffet sat on a tuffet.
3. Old Mac Donald had a ....

More difficult crosswords like the one below can be given to learners at a slightly higher level.

ACROSS

1 A person from another country (9)
6 A river in Egypt (4)
7 Don't forget to .... your watch. (4)
8 I don't believe you. You're pulling my .... (3)
9 To quarrel (5)
10 A flexible container used for carrying things (3)
12 It's .... heavy for me to carry. (3)
13 It's no .... crying over spilt milk. (3)

14 You'd better remind me in .... I forget. (4)
15 Either you come here .... I'll meet you there. (2)

Down

1 Wonderful; marvellous (9)
2 .... people believe in God. (9)
3 You're just .... time. (2)
4 The person next door (9)
5 Can you .... a bicycle? (4)
7 .... enjoyed ourselves at the party. (2)
8 The opposite of borrow (4)
11 If you mix black and white, you get .... (4)

Answers: Across 1. foreigner, 6. Nile, 7. wind, 8. leg, 9. argue, 10. bag, 12. too, 13. use, 14. case, 15. or; Down 1. fantastic, 2. religious, 3. in, 4. neighbour, 5. ride, 7. we, 8. lend, 11. grey

Crosswords can deal with a specific item of study, such as phrasal verbs.

Task-types

Matching

Matching tasks could be of different types, depending on the kind of items involved. The tasks shown here are just samples. Any number of matching tasks can be made up using different categories of words.

Synonyms

In the blanks alongside each word below, write a word that means almost the same as it. Choose your answers from the words in the box.

frighten .... hasten .... rescue ....
annoy .... yell ....

hurry scream vex save scare

Identification and matching

Diagrams (e.g., of a building or machine) and pictures (e.g., of a bird or animal, or the human body) can be used for this type of task.

Against each word, write the correct number that corresponds to the diagram on the right.

...... circumference
...... semicircle
...... radius
...... diameter
...... chord
...... arc

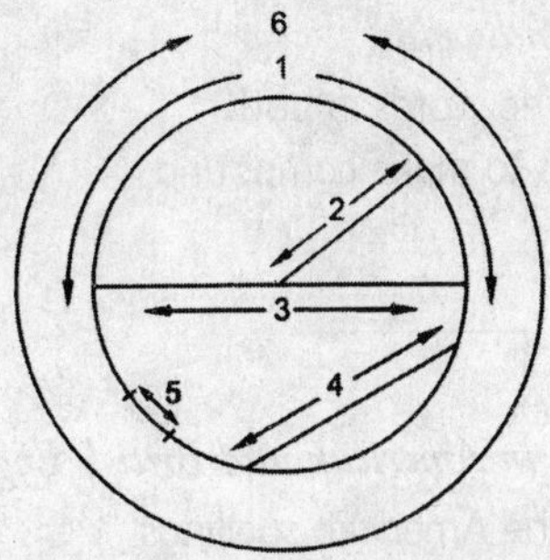

Idioms, similes and phrases

EXAMPLE 1: Complete the similes on the left by choosing words from the boxes on the right.

as heavy as	a bell
as tough as	gold
as good as	an eel
as slippery as	lead
as sound as	leather
as .... as clockwork	steady
as .... as a daisy	regular
as .... as a rock	smooth
as .... as glass	gentle
as .... as a lamb	fresh

EXAMPLE 2: Match the slang words in the left column with their meanings in the right column.

guts	alcoholic drink
booze	money
bread	courage
tripe	the police
fuzz	nonsense

Antonyms

Match the words on the left with words which mean the opposite from the column on the right.

tragic	mean
charitable	polite
arrest	repel
rude	release
attract	comic

Compound words

Match the words in both columns to make compound words.	hair	office
	birth	shade
	post	table
	sun	brush
	time	day

Spellings in American and British English

Match the American spellings with the British way of spelling the same words.	AMERICAN	BRITISH
	pajamas	sulphur
	check	kerb (noun)
	sulfur	doughnut
	draft	draught
	donut	pyjamas
	curb	cheque

Collocation of nouns and adjectives

Some words frequently go together, and, through long usage, such habitual groupings of words sound natural in English. For example, one says 'strong coffee' and not 'powerful coffee'. Combinations such as 'strong coffee' are known as *collocations.*

EXAMPLE 1: Underline the noun in the column on the right that best suits each adjective on the left.

excess	trouble, baggage, goods
violent	breeze, rain, storm
stubborn	walk, pout, attitude
civilised	behaviour, eating, talking
delicate	building, flower, waterfall

EXAMPLE 2: Underline the word that does not go with each adjective on the left.

expensive	equipment, education, learning
strong	coffee, meat, drink
enthusiastic	hero, supporter, admirer
prosperous	loss, businessman, years

BLANK FILLING

Blank filling can be of the supply type where the learner supplies his/her own word without any clues or support. For example:

Of all those on board the ...., Robinson Crusoe was the only one who was not .... He was washed up on the beach of a lovely .... When he had rested a little, Robinson got up from the sandy ...., and walked about. He felt very ....

This task can be made easier by giving the first letter of the expected vocabulary item.

The other main type of blank filling exercise is one where a choice of words is given. This is used more frequently at the school level as younger learners need help. For example:

Fill in the blanks, choosing one of the words in brackets.

The thief .... the bank. (robbed, stole)
He is trying to .... weight. (lose, loose)
He was .... enough to consult a doctor before taking the medicine. (sensitive, sensible)
They say .... never strikes twice. (lighting, lightning)
Our .... is very strict. (principal, principle)

SINGLE WORDS (GENERIC OR CLASS WORDS)

This task type relates to families of words, or words which belong to a single unit. For example, the words 'nurse', 'injection', 'bed', 'ward', 'matron' all belong to 'hospital'. Clues can be given and learners could be asked to supply the word. For example:

What do the following words belong to?

cloudy, rain, barometer, sunshine, wind	W _____ R
opera, waltz, symphony, conductor, concert	M ____ C

Learners could be asked to look up a dictionary for the words they do not know. If more help is needed, the family of words can be given, and the learners asked to match the list with the main word. For example:

subsidy, company, profit, shares, executive	make-up
skid, wheel, chauffeur, steering, mileage	business
eye shadow, lipstick, compact, perfume, mascara	vehicle

A few different variations of this task type are shown below.

Classification

At an earlier stage, learners could be given a list of words and asked to classify them under proper heads. For example:

Put the words below in the correct columns. Some items may go into more than one column.

fridge pillow bed sofa table chair oven carpet
book case telephone sink knives blanket night light

BEDROOM	KITCHEN	LIVING ROOM

Identification (odd one out)

The task involves picking out words that do not belong to a list and knowing how they are different. For example:

In the lists on the right, circle the word that does not fit. Say why you think it does not belong to the group.	army, brigade, fleet, regiment potatoes, rice, wheat, oats hotel, inn, tourist, motel father, mother, uncle, brother

Or the task could be one where the word which is not a near synonym is circled. For example:

Three of the words in each set mean more or less the same thing. Circle the odd one.	rubber, erase, cancel, delete finish, end, stop, start small, tiny, fry, little

Word family diagrams

These diagrams can be used at any stage of teaching vocabulary. They are based on associations and are an invaluable aid in vocabulary expansion.

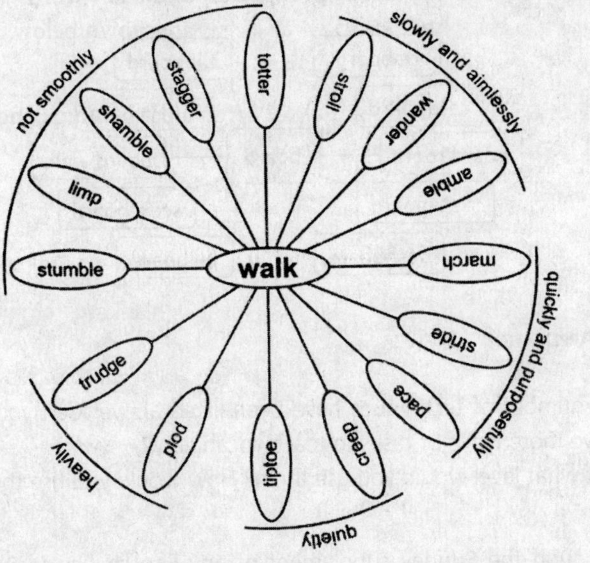

At the elementary level, the following type of diagram can be used.

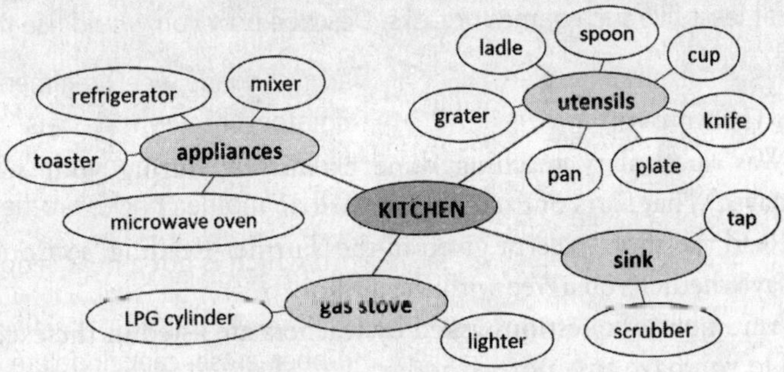

At a very advanced level, idiomatic expressions can be grouped around a key word.

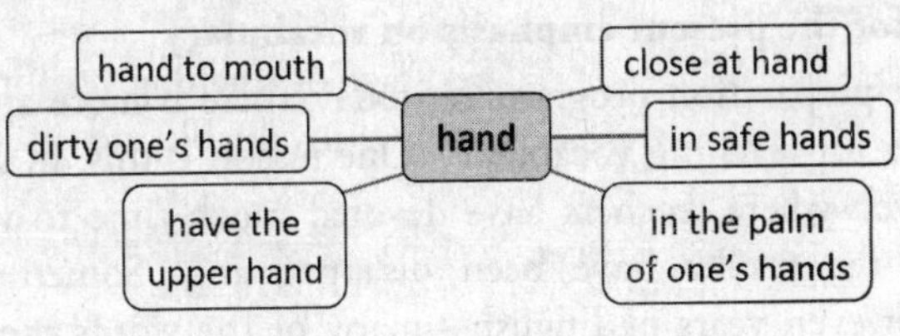

Compound words too can be grouped around a key word.

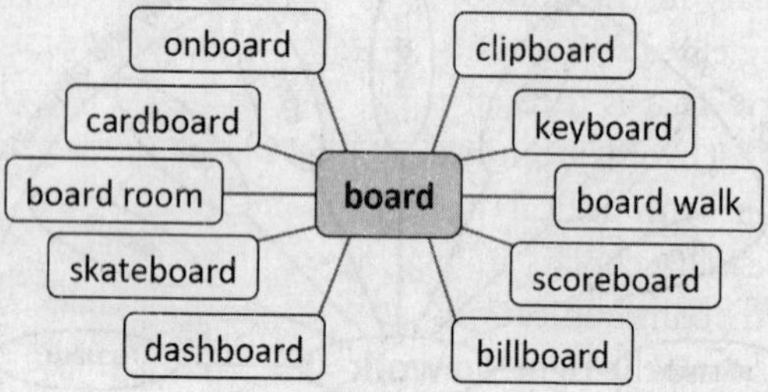

Application

Task 1

a. A number of techniques have been listed above. Can you think of two more types of tasks to teach vocabulary?

b. At what level would you use them? How would you use them?

Task 2

Go through the Sunday supplement of any English newspaper. In the children's section you will very often find vocabulary games and tasks. Find at least five such games or tasks. Describe how you would use them.

Think it over

1. Was vocabulary teaching done extensively during your school days? What sorts of exercises were used?
2. Read the short excerpt given in the 'Further Reading' section and say whether you agree with the author.
3. A number of questions asked by teachers are listed in the excerpt. Do you have any more to add?

Further reading

Reasons for the present emphasis on vocabulary

In teacher-preparation programmes today, there is more attention to techniques for teaching vocabulary. One reason is this: in many ESL classes, even where teachers have devoted much time to vocabulary teaching, the results have been disappointing. Sometimes—after months or even years of English—many of the words most needed have never been learned. Especially in countries where English is not the main language of communication, many teachers want more help with vocabulary instruction than they used to receive.

Something else also accounts for today's concern with the learning of vocabulary. That is the fact that scholars are taking a new interest in the study of word meanings. A number of research studies have recently dealt with lexical problems (problems related to words). Through research, scholars are finding that lexical problems frequently interfere with communication; communication breaks down when people do not use the right words.

Such discoveries by scholars do not surprise classroom teachers. Teachers have never doubted the value of learning vocabulary. They know how communication stops when learners lack the necessary words. They do not believe that the teaching of vocabulary should be delayed until the grammar is mastered. In the best classes, neither grammar nor vocabulary is neglected. There is thus no conflict between developing a firm command of grammar and learning the most essential words.

Today, therefore, professional journals and teachers' meetings often reflect the current concern for more effective vocabulary teaching. When teachers come together for professional discussions, they raise such questions as these:

- Which English words do students need most to learn?
- How can we make those words seem important to students?
- How can so many needed words be taught during the short time our students have for English?
- What can we do when a few members of the class already know words that the others need to learn?
- Why are some words easier than others to learn?
- Which aids to vocabulary teaching are available?
- How can we encourage students to take more responsibility for their own vocabulary learning?
- What are some good ways to find out how much vocabulary the students have actually learned?

Allen 1983

7

Teaching Aids

Teachers have always known that teaching aids can be used effectively to capture and sustain the attention of a class. Very often, these aids are used by teachers to put across or explain a concept in the best possible way to learners. These aids may vary from age-old ones like tamarind seeds and figures drawn on the ground with a stick to modern ones such as working models, video clips and touchscreen tablets.

In this chapter, we will discuss teaching aids in a systematic way. The teaching aids referred to here include traditional ones like the blackboard and the more modern ones like video.

The blackboard

The blackboard by itself, strictly speaking, is not a teaching aid, but it is something which can be transformed into a visual aid with the help of a piece of chalk.

Blackboards are no longer always 'black' and neither are they always made of board. Plastics and glass have increasingly replaced boards; though they are expensive, they last longer and require little maintenance. Colours now vary from the traditional black to green, blue, white or even pale grey. Special felt-tipped pens are used with white or grey boards. In places where even the traditional blackboard cannot be afforded, a space on the wall is simply painted over to provide a chalkboard surface.

Whatever the material of the blackboard, the techniques used by a teacher are the same. Blackboard work can mean either writing or drawing. In language teaching, the spoken is reinforced by the written (or vice versa), as the word (or concept) is reinforced by the picture. So, it is important that blackboard work be done effectively by the teacher. The criteria for effective blackboard work are listed below.

NEATNESS AND TIDINESS

A scrawl on the blackboard is neither effective nor useful, and can often become counter-productive.

THINK IT OVER

Given below are a few samples of blackboard writing. Study them and give your comments on each of them.

a) 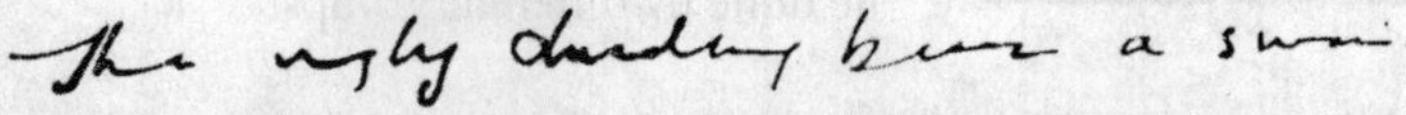

b) 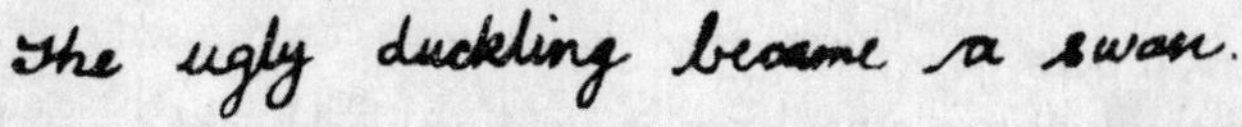

c) 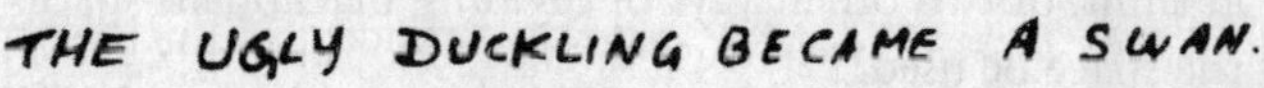

d) 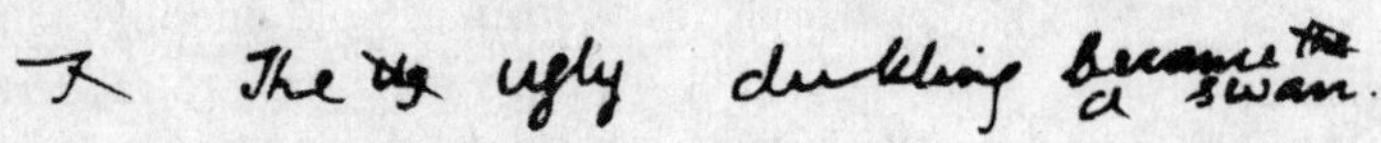

e) 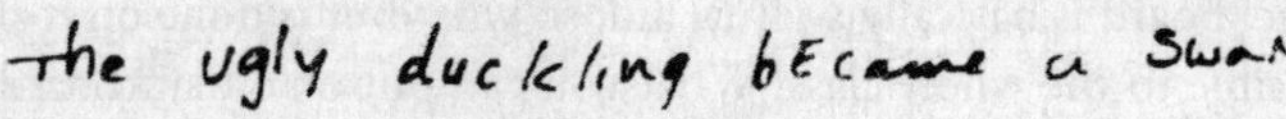

f) 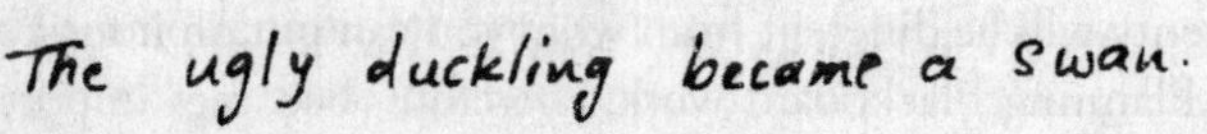

JUDICIOUS USE OF SPACE

A crowded blackboard is not an aid but a deterrent to learning. Learners will not know what part of the blackboard work to focus on. To make optimal use of blackboard space, a teacher should plan before each lesson how the space will be used. Four of the many ways in which a blackboard can be divided are given below.

This pattern is useful for developing lessons. The right-hand column can be used to write down new items. These are not erased throughout the lesson. The remaining sections are used for visuals/other work.

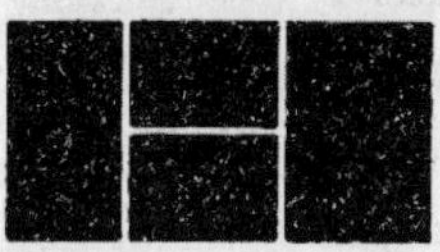

The H-model divides the blackboard into four sections: one for visuals; one for tables, lists, etc.; one for planned work; and one for learner responses.

A two-part division is useful for guided compositions. One part is used for clues (visual/verbal), and the other for learner responses and lesson development.

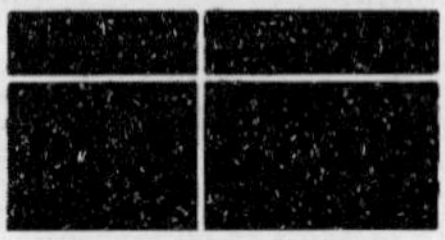

This is ideal for setting up classroom activities (pair/group work). Each section has the task/input needed for the work to be done by different groups.

Think it over

Can you think of two other ways of dividing blackboard space? How would the space be used?

Visibility

A blackboard is basically a visual aid, so whatever is done on it should be visible to the whole class. What you can put on a blackboard for a class of twenty will be different from what you can put on it for a class of eighty. Planning blackboard work, therefore, becomes important. Visibility is as important for pictures as it is for writing. It is always better to draw pictures in bold lines than use fussy details, which take time and can be seen by only the first two rows of learners.

Think it over

Given below are two samples of blackboard work. Say which work is for a large class and which one is for a small class.

1. A dog once stole a piece of meat from a butcher's. As it was running away, it came to a bridge. It looked down and saw its reflection in the water.
2. dog / stole / a piece of meat / butcher's / running away / came to a bridge / looked down / saw reflection in water

In what way is the blackboard work different? What has the teacher done? Why?

Accuracy

If we make mistakes while speaking, we can correct them or gloss over them. We cannot do this when we write, especially on a blackboard. Each small error will be highlighted. What is even more damaging is that learners may copy down these errors into their notebooks. A teacher who wants to use the blackboard effectively will take extra care to put up only correct things on the blackboard.

THINK IT OVER

Can you think of four important areas, besides spelling, where errors on the blackboard can occur?

SMOOTHNESS OF EXECUTION

A teacher who fumbles at the blackboard does not make a good impression. Neither does the teacher who takes a long time to write on the blackboard. (The class often gets restless.) The advocates of the italic style of handwriting have identified three parameters for effective writing: legibility, speed and beauty. These hold good for all blackboard work, both in writing and in pictures.

Pictures

These can be drawn either on the blackboard, on chart paper or on cutouts.

MEDIA

Drawing pictures on the *blackboard* may seem difficult and even impossible for many teachers. But there is a way out. Simple stick figures (matchstick figures) can be attempted successfully by everybody. A bit of practice gives smoothness and speed. Given below are some examples:

If a teacher masters the rudiments of blackboard drawing, then a variety of activities can be done in the class—from riddles to picture compositions. For example:

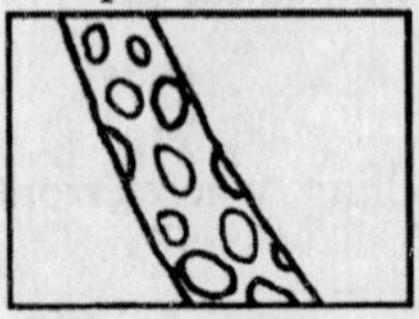

Speaking activity
Question: What is this?
Answer: A giraffe passing by a window.

Think of two other activities you can do using blackboard drawing.

Charts are easy to make and use. Unlike blackboard drawings, these can be displayed for a longer time. If a chart has to be used for the whole class, visibility becomes the primary criteria. (Letters/characters that are two and a half inches high are visible up to thirty feet.) Pictures must be clear and unambiguous. An example of a useful chart is one which has the signs the teacher uses for correcting writing work.

ʎ	Word missing
Sp	Spelling mistake
Gr	Wrong grammar
//	Start a new paragraph
??	What do you mean?

Flash cards are approximately ten by twelve inches in size. They are flashed before a class to

- emphasise or bring home an idea
- teach reading (also speed reading)
- teach sounds
- play games

The use of flash cards can be divided roughly into five steps.

1. prepare learner (by introducing item/topic)
2. present flash cards
3. apply information
4. test learner
5. review

For example, flash cards can be used in the following manner:

(Input) John drinks coffee every day.

(Teacher flashes picture of John with a cold drink.)

(Output) But he's drinking cola now.

Flash cards can have a picture on one side and the text on the other. This makes it easy for the teacher to check learner understanding.

Flash cards can be colour coded too. Thus, words belonging to different parts of speech could be put on cards of different colours. For example, articles can be printed on white cards; nouns, on pink; verbs, green; and adverbs on blue cards. Learners choose one card from each category and make a sentence, such as 'The bird sang sweetly'.

A *flannel board* is a stationary surface covered with a rough flannel cloth, usually dark in colour. Pictures, cards and sentence strips backed by a piece of rough sandpaper are stuck on these boards. (The sandpaper adheres to the flannel.) The flannel board is useful at all levels of teaching.

At the lower levels, words are taught in the following way:

1. A card with 'at' is stuck on the board.

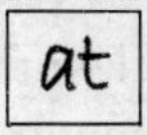

2. The teacher says the word, and the class repeats it.
3. The teacher starts introducing different consonant sounds and sticks the relevant cards next to it.

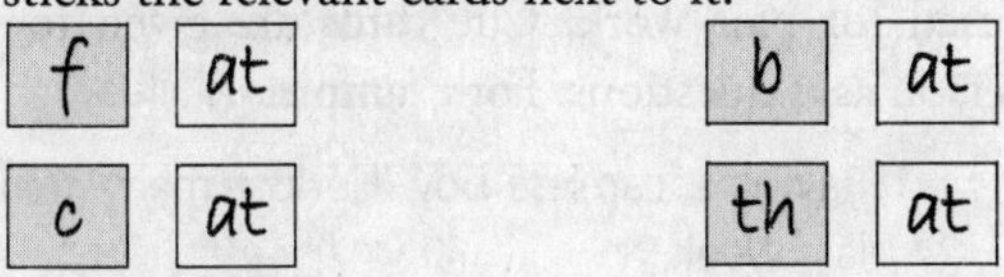

4. The class repeats the words—connecting the sounds and the graphics.

This way of teaching is also called the phonic method, and these cards are called 'phonic cards'.

At a later stage, sentences of a paragraph can be stuck jumbled up on the flannel board. In groups, learners work out the right order and reorder the paragraph on the flannel boards. Other groups react—either agreeing or not agreeing with the order and giving reasons for doing so.

A flannel board can also be used to teach an aspect of language, for example, ways of expressing the future. Each segment of the circle on the right can be put on the flannel board separately, one after the other, and the final pie chart will present a summary of the lesson.

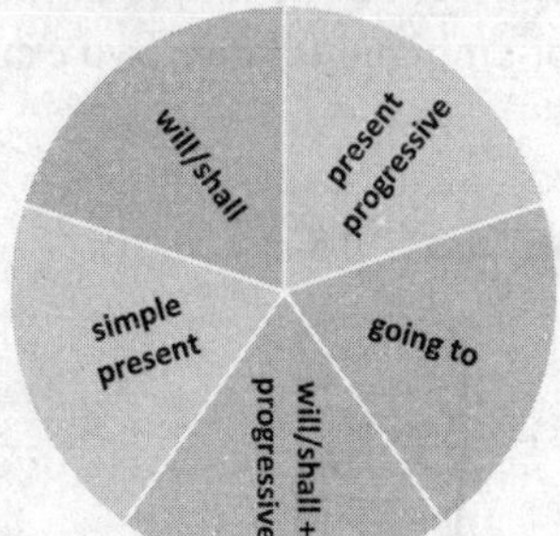

Visibility

Sometimes, teachers find beautiful pictures in magazines and newspapers and plan to use it in their teaching. Very often, they fail because they forget that what one person can see need not necessarily be visible to the whole class. Thus, however attractive pictures from newspapers and magazines may be, they can be seen clearly only by the first few rows of the class. So it is important to bear in mind the important factor of visibility when using such pictures.

However, even medium to small pictures can be exploited successfully for pair or group work in which the picture is passed round a small group or when only two persons have to work with it. Here, the choice of the picture, rather than its visibility, is important. Pictures should be chosen not only because they are colourful and pretty, but also because they are relevant to the task.

Pictures can be used for pair work. Cue cards are given to one person. The other person asks questions. For example:

Teacher	Ravi is a careless boy. He lost many things last week.
Student 1	What did Ravi lose on Monday?
Student 2	A pencil.
Student 1	What did he lose on Tuesday?
Student 2	A book.

Talking about pictures

Talking about pictures is another way in which pictures can be used as a teaching aid. Learners can be given picture inputs to talk about. This activity helps develop oral skills and in many cases, vocabulary. The pictures can be simple in the earlier stages, and become more complex or ambiguous later. Two examples are given below.

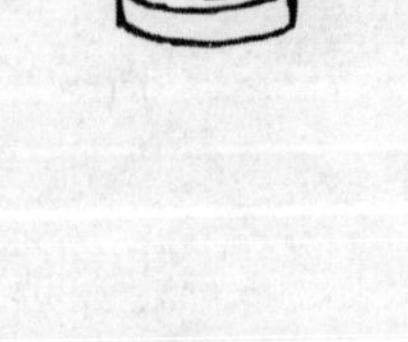

Two ways to get learners to talk about pictures are:

- *Memory games*: A picture is shown to the learners, who have to remember as many of its details as possible.
- *Narration*: Pictures can be very effectively used as input for eliciting short narrations practised in groups. For example:

Set A	HOTEL	GIRL	FOOD ITEM	CINEMA	BICYCLE
Set B	MALL	BOY	FOOD ITEM	PARK	BUS
Set C	CAFÉ	FRIEND	FOOD ITEM	DISCO	CAR

Members of a group draw a set of five cards and narrate the sequence of events in the cards. They can also change the sequence of cards for a different kind of effect. For example, the narration may be like the following:

Yesterday, I went to Hotel Ritz on a bicycle. I met a girl there. She and I had fried potatoes, and later we went to the cinema.

Think of two other activities you can do using pictures.

Realia

In language teaching, *realia* refers to

> actual objects and items which are brought into a classroom as examples or as aids to be talked or written about and used in teaching. Realia may include such things as photographs, articles of clothing, and kitchen objects.
>
> *Longman Dictionary of Applied Linguistics* 1985

Realia is an important part of language teaching at the primary level, used:

- to present vocabulary
- to present new structures
- for drama/role play
- for language games

Realia, however, is not useful at all levels and in all classes. A teacher must be judicious in selecting this kind of aid. Also, using realia does not necessarily make the lesson effective. Too much realia clutters up the lesson and the classroom.

Projectors

Projection technology in the classroom has come a long way, from lamp-illuminated overhead projectors which made use of transparencies, to computer-based LCD projectors, to the interactive smartboards of today. As a teaching aid, projectors have always been rather expensive. Therefore, very few schools or institutions invest in it. But those who have it find that it can be very useful, especially in large classes.

The first advantage of using overhead projection is that as the screen is quite big, the projection can be seen by everyone in the class. Secondly, the teacher need not waste time writing on the blackboard; the matter being projected is prepared *before* the class. The use of this aid thus has an additional advantage—it ensures that the teacher plans the lesson. However, care should be taken to ensure that what is displayed on the screen is essential material, for example the major categories under which a subject is being considered, the summary of a lesson, or a diagrammatic representation of the topic under discussion.

Audio recordings

Equipment for the recording and playback of sounds—whether tape recorders, handheld dictation devices, CD players, computers, or apps on smartphones—can be found in most schools. They are relatively inexpensive, and allow audio to be stored and played via a wide variety of media, both analogue and digital. Internet connectivity allows access to an even wider range of listening materials on numerous topics in the form of podcasts (digital recordings of discussions, lectures, news, etc. available for download).

As a language teacher, it is important to think of the uses to which audio materials can be put. This is because the use of any audiovisual aid should be judged according to the answer to the question 'What can the aid do which a teacher in the classroom cannot do?'. Audio recording and playback devices can be used for a variety of activities. Some are listed below:

- *Listening to sounds, words, sentences and conversations:* A listening task will put learners in touch with almost all aspects of spoken English, and over a period of time they can learn to use what they have acquired through listening.
- *Listening and note making:* Authentic bits of a lecture, talk or conversation are played, and learners asked to make notes.

- *Reading aloud practice:* Bits of the prescribed text can be recorded. The learners can either listen to the recording and mimic it, or read the text and listen to the audio version. The whole class can then discuss both the readings in terms of specific aspects. For example: Where did the speaker pause in the audio version? Where did the learner pause? Why?
- *Discussions:* There are pre-recorded clips of sound effects available on the internet. The teacher plays some sound effects, and the class, either in groups or pairs, discusses (what, where, when, how, why) the sounds they have heard. Since this is an open-ended task, a variety of interpretations are possible.
- *Listen to yourself:* With prior consent and cooperation of the class, the teacher positions a recording device strategically to record, for example, a discussion activity. This is an effective way of making the learners aware of what their production of spoken English is like. This in turn helps both the learner and the teacher to diagnose problem areas (either at the sound level or at the pragmatic level) and come up with remedial measures.
- *Recording dialogues and conversations:* Another activity that the class can do is to write short dialogues or conversations which they present to the class. The dialogues can be recorded and later discussed.

When using external audio sources, it is important to remember a few practical points:

- Can the whole class hear the audio clearly?
- If an external speaker is being used, are the facilities for providing power reliable?
- Is there any back-up facility if the power fails?
- Is there noise pollution from other sources (the noise of traffic, for example)?
- Is the quality of the audio of an acceptable standard?

Besides this, the teacher must plan at which point in the lesson she/he will use the audio material—at the beginning, middle or end of the lesson.

THINK IT OVER

1. Should learners be exposed only to the teacher's English? Why, or why not?

2. Given below are a few statements. Decide along with a partner whether you agree or disagree with them, or whether you would want to modify them. State your reasons.
   a. An audio clip does not add anything significant to a class.
   b. A printed text helps learners learn the language more effectively than an audio resource.
   c. For conversations, a teacher using glove puppets would be more effective than an audio recording.
   d. It is important to provide an unvarying model when teaching speech.
   e. We cannot check whether learners are listening actively when an audio clip is played in the class.

The language laboratory

This consists of a system which makes use of voice recording and playback to provide individualised language-learning facilities. A typical language laboratory has booths for individual learners, each equipped with a media player, a headset, a microphone and a voice recorder. Only basic controls (such as play, pause, rewind or record) are provided to learners. Learners can work through tasks at their own pace. The booths are connected to a control panel, and the teacher supervising the language laboratory session can plug into any of the booths to listen in and provide help if required.

The advantage of such a setup is that every student gets more time to practise listening and speaking. (In regular classrooms, the more the number of students, the less time each individual gets to speak the language being learnt.)

A typical language laboratory lesson has the following pattern:

a. The learner listens to the sample or master recording.
b. The learner repeats what she/he has heard, or does the task.
c. The learner plays back the tape and listens to her/his recording.

This follows the pattern 'stimulus → response → feedback', a pattern advocated by the structural methodologists.

Some variations are introduced in these programmes, though the basic pattern remains the same.

Variation 1

a. The learner listens (to the model).

b. The learner speaks.
c. The learner listens (to the model).

Variation 2

a. This is the same as above, but there is a fourth step:
b. The learner repeats it.

Variation 3

a. The learner listens (to the model).
b. The learner identifies the sound (on a task sheet).
c. The learner practises it.

Variation 4

a. The learner listens (to a dialogue).
b. The learner answers questions.
c. The learner listens to the right answer.

Variation 5

a. The learner listens (to a dialogue).
b. The learner takes role 1.
c. The learner takes role 2.
d. The learner plays back the whole.

THINK IT OVER

In what ways is the language laboratory different from the portable tape recorder? What special features does it have?

Television and radio

The immense popularity of radio (in the early decades of the twentieth century) and television (from the 1950s onwards) lead to on-air classes—language-learning broadcasts that were created specifically for these powerful forms of media.

Such specially produced television and radio programmes have certain limitations. The broadcast time is fixed and it is generally a one-way process. Teaching, as we know, is a two-way process.

However, on-air classes are not the only way that television and radio can be used as teaching aids. Any content in the target language (whether films, programmes or even news) that a learner finds interesting or enjoyable can lead to the picking up of the language's rhythms, intonation and vocabulary through both active and passive listening. Reading subtitles can reinforce what the learner listens to.

Nowadays, interactive television, which allows the viewer to engage with the programme by making choices or taking actions that modify the content of the broadcast, is being used for teaching purposes in a limited way. If successful, it may well be the next step in language learning through television.

Video

Video is another modern technology which is increasingly being brought into use for teaching. Video has all of the advantages of television programmes. At the same time, unlike television lessons, the teacher can decide when to play video content; it can be paused, rewound and replayed at will by the teacher. With the increasing availability of high-speed mobile internet, streaming video has become yet another tool in the teacher's arsenal. Camcorders and smartphones with video cameras have made it possible for individuals to shoot their own films.

Video can be used in a classroom in a number of ways. For example, during a lesson on the use of English for social purposes, a party scene could be shown on mute. People are seen smiling, nodding, shaking hands, etc. Learners are asked to supply the dialogue. After learners have finished the task, they can listen to the actual conversation and compare it with their production.

The possibilities which audiovisual aids offer are enormous. Audiovisual aids are more often than not attractive, and a teacher might feel that using audiovisual aids would make the lesson effective. But, like all teaching aids, the purposes to which the aid is put, the objectives of using the aid, and its cost-effectiveness should be borne in mind. It would indeed be very foolish to spend twelve hours and a few hundred rupees on preparing an audiovisual aid which would be used for just five minutes in the class. So a set of criteria for evaluating teaching aids in terms of effectiveness should be evolved and used.

The six main criteria for evaluating effectiveness are:

- cost
- ease of manipulation of the equipment
- compatibility with the size of the class

- flexibility of use (that is, can it be used for different purposes?)
- control status (that is, can it be controlled by the user?)
- preparation time

The effectiveness of the audiovisual aid should be reflected in the behaviour of the learners. The teacher could ask herself/himself these questions:

- Are learners interested?
- Has the use of the aid resulted in learning efficiency?
- Have certain identified deficiencies been overcome?
- Have test results improved?

If at least two of the above questions get a positive answer, then the teaching aid has been effective.

SECTION SUMMARY

- Audiovisual aids are important in teaching. When utilised well, they can increase learner engagement and improve learning efficiency.
- A set of criteria for evaluating audiovisual aids is necessary. These include, among others, cost, ease of use, and positive learner outcomes.

DID YOU UNDERSTAND?

1. What are the things you have to remember while using the blackboard?
2. How many types of visual aids are there?
3. Write short notes on:
   a. flash cards
   b. flannel boards
   c. magazine pictures
4. To what uses can an overhead projector be put?
5. What should be the criteria for using audiovisual aids?
6. Complete the following table:

Teaching aid	Cost	Preparation of materials	Control	Uses
blackboard	affordable	teacher	teacher control	
television set	affordable	only professionals; studio required	outside control	
voice recorder				

APPLICATION

TASK 1

Write and prepare a listening and note-taking task for class 9 learners. Say what should be recorded (including instructions), where the recording will be paused, etc.

Decide how you will check the task—will you record the answers or will the teacher come into the picture?

TASK 2

Prepare a language laboratory drill for the *if* clause, type 1. State clearly:

a. the pattern you will use
b. what goes on the teacher's audio resource
c. what the learners have to do

TASK 3

Given alongside is a picture. Devise tasks which will exploit the picture. Mention the level of the learners, the number of learners present, and the type of activity (group work/pair work/whole class activity).

TASK 4

Write out the story of the fox and the grapes using stick figures.

Information and communication technology

The use of teaching aids has become more technology oriented with the introduction of computers. Information and communication technology (ICT) refers to all technology, both hardware and software, that allows people to access, use and transfer information through modes of telecommunication (such as the internet and wired/wireless networks). ICT has come to play an increasingly large role in the field of education by supporting and enriching the processes of teaching and learning in many ways.

ICT IN EDUCATION

ICT can be used both for teaching lessons and for managing the class (lesson planning, task assignment, assessment, report generation, etc.).

The most widespread use of ICT in education is in e-learning. E-learning refers to the use of electronic media to access online (internet-based) or offline learning materials. The common modes of e-learning include the following:

- Massive open online courses (MOOCs) are structured courses that are available on the internet, often for free and sometimes for a fee; for example, an online teacher-training course for professional development, mapped to globally recognised standards. These are 'on-demand' classes: students learn at their own pace. Course materials, typically in the form of lectures or presentations recorded by qualified instructors, are available online, and the students have to work through these. Most such courses have assignments and an examination at the end. Paid courses also include feedback from instructors via e-mail, interactions with teachers and fellow course-mates via chat, and certification on achieving a passing grade.
- Some institutes of formal education have begun offering online classes for undergraduate and postgraduate degrees. These colleges and universities replicate the experience of in-person classrooms in a virtual environment. Students log in to classes at specific times to watch professors deliver live lectures. The course works more or less in the same way as a traditional course with assignments, tests, etc., except that course materials are accessed electronically and tests conducted online. Communication between students and teachers happen via e-mail and chat (text or video).
- In the corporate world, e-learning is sometimes employed for training in specific technical skills. Such training is usually delivered through software that is customised to suit the needs of a particular company or an industry; for example, spoken English practice scenarios for newly employed call-centre executives.
- Online learning opportunities can also be in the form of live virtual workshops and webinars, accessed via video conferencing or live-streaming digital video platforms; for example, a workshop on creative writing.
- Courseware can be shared via a local area network (LAN), a system that allows connected computers within a room or a building to communicate with each other. Work produced by students can be uploaded to the LAN and assessed by the teacher.

- In addition to the above examples of online learning, offline modes of e-learning can supplement traditional in-person teaching. Digital libraries of e-books, recorded audio and video lectures, and similar course materials are valuable resources that can be shared quickly and accessed through digital devices. Certain lessons or even entire courses can also be made available via CDs and DVDs.

ICT doesn't just help learners, but also those who build and manage courses and training programmes. The best example of the use of ICT in this regard is a learning management system (LMS). These are software applications that help teachers, educators and administrators develop, deliver, and track courses and learning modules. Such systems even have provision for administrative activities such as admissions, fee collection and sending out of information. LMSs are used not only by educational institutes and administrators of online courses, but also by corporate organisations that utilise LMSs to train employees.

An LMS can aid in lesson planning (for example, by modifying and repurposing existing lessons) and assessment (for example, through surveys and quizzes). Its in-built tools can also analyse data on students' strengths and weaknesses based on test results. Academic management systems can therefore help teachers become more efficient in a number of ways.

Advantages

ICT brings many potential advantages to education.

- ICT can provide new ways of teaching and learning a subject through the use of multimedia content. For example, lessons for children can be presented through cartoon characters and music. Young learners invariably enjoy these sessions. Automated spaced repetition can be used for building and retaining vocabulary in older learners (in place of traditional flash cards). Such methods don't merely clarify the material being taught but present it in ways that spark interest and reduce boredom. This increases students' engagement levels and makes them more attentive.
- When used effectively, technology can encourage and motivate students to take charge of their learning. (This is particularly true for well-designed interactive tools that promote initiative and active participation, because these make learners invest in the learning process.) Being more involved is a desirable quality to nurture as it has a positive impact on learners' achievements.

- Students often have different styles of learning and pick up knowledge at different speeds. Technology can provide opportunities for learners to learn at their own pace and in a personalised manner that helps them understand the subject better than a one-size-fits-all approach.
- Teaching and learning resources delivered through ICT can usually be updated more quickly and easily than content disseminated through traditional media (such as print, which can take a lot more time and resources to revise).
- Online courses and digital tools can promote increased collaboration between learners. Even those separated by continents can work together on projects and learn from each other.
- ICT can lead to greater access to education, especially for learners held back by traditional barriers such as gender, geography or distance, lack of economic resources, physical disabilities, time constraints, and so on. Open courseware and the abundance and variety of free resources online have made knowledge affordable and accessible. Tools such as e-learning can thus result in a more inclusive educational system—and a more inclusive society.
- An offshoot of the use of ICT in education is that it prepares learners for the computer-centric world of the twenty-first century. Technology has come to dominate every aspect of life (including essential services), and engaging with ICT helps integrate learners into the knowledge economy of today by teaching them to use and produce information effectively. It has also been argued that learning to use ICT competently promotes higher-order thinking skills such as planning and analysis, which are key skills to encourage in every learner.
- From an administrative point of view, ICT facilitates better management of the learning environment, and can make processes such as lesson delivery, testing, grading, etc. smoother and more flexible.

Challenges

One must also be aware of the challenges involved in employing ICT in education. E-learning has made remarkable progress in the past few decades, but there are still several factors that prevent its wide adoption.

- E-learning requires computers and sophisticated infrastructure, which many schools and colleges in India still do not have. These are often too expensive to purchase and maintain, especially in the Indian context.
- E-learning expects students to be responsible learners who need to work on their own. Web-based tools and courses in particular require a certain degree of self-discipline because of the immense potential for distraction on the internet.
- A computer is impersonal; it is not like having a teacher in a classroom setting. Peer interaction also helps the learning process, but this is often missing in e-learning.
- E-learning is harder to implement effectively at the elementary level, as children are being taught concepts, which can be very difficult to teach via the computer. Other areas where e-learning might fall short include practical work and work that needs to be assessed subjectively. Educators would need to employ a more hands-on approach in such cases.
- It is often difficult to gauge the authenticity of a student's work since technology makes it very easy to reproduce and pass off other people's work as one's own.
- There are apprehensions that long-term reliance on audiovisual content in study materials may shorten the attention spans of learners.
- Finally, there are valid concerns that the use of ICT may lead to greater exclusion in education for those who do not have access to ICT tools and resources. This is particularly true in societies (such as India) with large income disparities. Those at risk of being excluded by this 'digital divide' include not only learners from economically weaker sections of society, but also (among others) learners who don't belong to dominant language groups, those less familiar with technology, and those with special needs.

The disadvantages of e-learning are being reduced with the advances being made in ICT. The modes of e-learning, too, are constantly being tweaked to suit the needs of both teachers and learners.

- The prices of computers are coming down every year. Besides, most government grants to educational institutions today include money for computers, and various schemes have been launched by different governments and funding bodies to equip schools and colleges with computers.

- The infrastructure required to run computer labs is becoming simpler. Further, the component parts of modern computers also take up less space than those of earlier models.
- Face-to-face interaction is a major advantage of conventional classroom-based teaching. To incorporate this experience, many e-learning courses offer 'blended learning'—some work on the computer combined with some physical face-to-face teaching in brick-and-mortar classrooms. This also takes care of peer interaction. Where blended learning cannot be offered, e-courses offer live chat sessions with tutors or teachers. These have been made possible thanks to high-speed internet and video live-streaming. The other, and perhaps more expensive, option is video conferencing.
- It has been accepted that very young children need to learn in 'live' rather than 'virtual' situations. Therefore e-learning is not done extensively at the elementary level. However, children are encouraged to use computers to practise what they have learnt. For example, if a child has had a lesson on prepositions in the classroom, she/he can go back to an e-course on the topic and do exercises on it.

ICT IN ELT

The computer is becoming more and more central to our work and also in our private lives. Computer skills are becoming a very important part of the curriculum, even at the school level. The result of this is that topics like 'How to write an e-mail' and 'Presentation skills' have become a part of the syllabus that English teachers need to deal with. The importance of computers in ELT can be seen in the number of publications that have come out in the past few years on topics such as 'Using computers to teach English' and 'Using the internet to teach English'.

ICT can be a useful tool in the teaching and learning of English. Consider, for example, a common scenario in an English class: producing a piece of writing. The problem most teachers face when it comes to writing is the reluctance of students to edit their work before submitting it. Perhaps this is because the teacher is seen as a 'correction machine', or because students find it tedious to rewrite whole chunks of writing by hand on paper. A computer is of great help here because the draft can be revised with regard to its punctuation, spelling, grammar, and even the organisation of the complete piece, without much trouble. Students' awareness of the mechanisms of writing can be raised through the use of word processing tools.

There are a number of ways in which technology can help in English language teaching. Some examples are listed below.

- The abundance of written matter, audio, video and digital tools available on the internet may be the best alternative to learning by immersion for many learners in India. (Adding to this is the fact that English is often the default language of most ICT devices.)
- In addition to vast quantities of searchable information on every conceivable topic, the internet also makes available a wide range of prompts and other stimuli for classroom discussion and written production.
- Engaging multimedia content may motivate young learners to complete tasks that they may otherwise procrastinate on or shirk altogether (such as practise exercises or repetitive tasks).
- Audio books provide a wealth of listening practise along with good (and varied) models of stress, intonation and pronunciation. They also serve as useful tools for strengthening the second-language abilities of learners who have reading disabilities.
- Mobile apps are particularly good at gamifying[1] the learning of vocabulary and structures, tapping into behavioural science to spur faster language acquisition in learners across ages.

As in other courses, the development of e-learning programmes is cyclical as represented in the figure below.

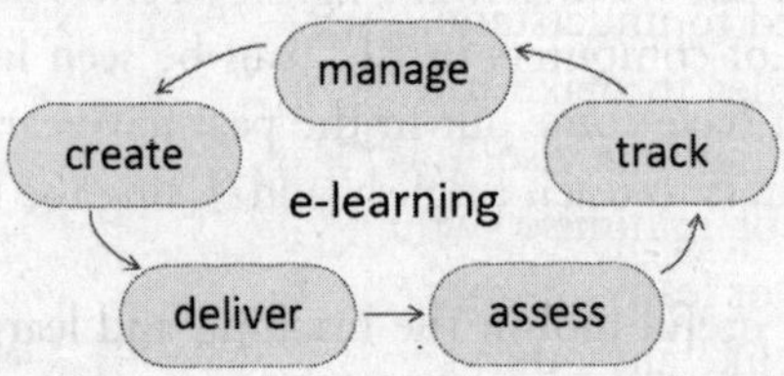

The role of the teacher

It has always been maintained that English language teaching is a skill-based subject, not a content-based one. This is true even today with

[1] To 'gamify' is to apply typical elements of a game (such as point scoring, competition with others, etc.) to an activity in order to increase engagement with the said activity.

the proliferation of ICT learning tools. In the teaching of English, the skills of using the language are more important than the content, and the English teacher has to play the unique role of the one imparting these skills.

Take, for example, doing research for writing. Students have ready access to vast amounts of information through CDs, the internet, etc. But CDs or the internet become useful only when users know *how* to search for the information, and *what* to look for. Without these two skills, the use of ICT to search for information in oceans of irrelevant and unreliable data becomes confusing and ineffective. Here is where the teacher comes in with non-technological skills—namely, the skills students need to deploy to clarify what one is looking for, and then locate, narrow down and select reliable information efficiently.

Thus, non-technological skills (such as lesson planning, etc.) are required to make the technology work effectively in service of learning needs. However, working with such aids does necessitate basic computer literacy on the part of the teacher. Where ICT is put into use, teachers will have to be willing to upgrade their skills to make the best use of the tools available to them. Without a certain level of familiarity and comfort with the tools at hand (and an open mind regarding their use), it would be difficult to successfully integrate ICT into English language teaching in ways that enhance the curriculum and the learning process. Depending on the situation and the tool used, the teacher may need to give up some control to allow for greater learner autonomy; her/his role thus shifts from that of an instructor to a facilitator.

Teachers need to understand the advantages imparted by available ICT aids in order to make use of their strengths in supplementing classroom teaching, *and* also understand their disadvantages in order to circumvent or minimise them so that they do not interfere with either teaching or learning.

Technology, like any other teaching aid, is as useful as the teacher makes it. While the latest technology may open up exciting possibilities, it still requires non-technical skills to make it contribute effectively and meaningfully towards learning objectives. No teaching aid can be a substitute for the teacher's knowledge of the subject and her/his teaching abilities. The use of any technology needs to be supported by careful planning; else, it becomes a redundant piece of equipment in the teaching–learning process.

Section summary

- ICT is a catch-all term for computers, communication devices and software applications used to store, process and transmit information.
- A number of online and offline tools are available now for e-learning, as are tools for the coordination and management of education.
- ICT offers teachers and students new and engaging ways of teaching and learning that transcend barriers to education and are efficient in terms of time and cost. The use of ICT in education can foster learner autonomy and prepare students for a digital future.
- The limitations of using ICT in education include high initial set-up costs, improper implementation, and the possible widening of the digital divide.
- The effective use of ICT in ELT requires judicious planning on the part of educators to figure out ways in which these new aids can add value to the teaching–learning process.

Did you understand?

1. What are the possible benefits and drawbacks of using computers to teach language?
2. What skills can students develop by using ICT tools when learning?
3. What is 'blended learning'?
4. Can e-learning be implemented in schools in your area? Why or why not?

Application

Task 1

Two pages from the website of an online course are given on pages 198–199. Go through the pages and answer these questions:

a. Who do you think is this course meant for? What evidence do you have?

b. What do you think is the function of the following buttons/links? (i) Sitemap, (ii) Search, (iii) Help, (iv) Previous
c. Does this lesson require a teacher or is the student expected to learn on her/his own? Justify your answer.
d. Is there any opportunity for interaction with other learners?

TASK 2

Take a passage from a textbook. Design an e-learning module for either reading or vocabulary. (You could refer to the chapter 'Techniques of teaching English' for ideas.)

- For which level will you design the module?
- Cartoon figures, stick figures, pictures, diagrams and even animation can be used in an e-learning module. Do you think you will want to illustrate your module?

Workplace ESL Online

Sign In

Register

Your one-stop portal for English at the workplace

Lessons | Resources | Forum | Sitemap   Search

Lessons

Searching for a Job

- Understanding job advertisements
- Crafting your résumé
- Résumé and interview-related terms and acronyms
- Describing yourself
- Interview-related dialogues I
- Interview-related dialogues II
- Body language

Starting Work

- Job descriptions
- Introducing yourself to colleagues
- Workplace-related vocabulary I
- Formal English at the workplace I
- Talking about your work
- Safety at work

Getting Ahead

- Workplace-related vocabulary II
- Formal English at the workplace II
- Meetings I
- Presentations I
- Water cooler conversations
- Meetings II
- Presentations II
- Networking in English

Test Yourself!

- Vocabulary
- Quizzes
- Worksheets

Workplace ESL Online

SIGN IN

REGISTER

Your one-stop portal for English at the workplace

Lessons | Resources | Forum | Sitemap   Search

Talking about your work

PRE-LESSON ACTIVITY — Expand this section

LISTEN

Watch the video below of Amir, Sonia and Rithu at a café.
Listen carefully to the language they use for talking about their jobs.

Tips

Quiz

Help

READ AND SPEAK — Expand this section

Now read the transcript of their conversation.
Practise saying aloud the useful phrases that have been underlined.

TASK 1 — Expand this section

TASK 2 — Expand this section

TASK 3 — Expand this section

WRITE — Expand this section

Write two paragraphs about what you do for a living and where you work.
Do you like your job? Why or why not?

Previous   Next

8

Testing

What is a test?

A test is a procedure for measuring ability, knowledge or performance. A test is used not only in academic courses, but also elsewhere; it is used in situations where the performance of people or things needs to be measured and discriminated.

Types of tests

In the teaching–learning situation, tests are used for various purposes. The type of test varies according to the purpose for which it is used. The important types of tests are:

Placement tests

They are forward-looking tests designed to group learners at the start of a course. These tests deal with the general abilities of the learners rather than specific skills. For example, the director of an institute teaching French might want to know the general abilities of learners in French before allocating a learning programme—elementary, intermediate or advanced—or a course in spoken French rather than in written French.

Placement tests are fairly brief as they have to be marked quickly. As general abilities are assessed, a variety of test types (or a battery) is used; for example, dictation, a cloze test, or an interview.

Diagnostic tests

As the name implies, these tests are designed to diagnose whether the learner has learnt something well or whether she/he needs special help in learning an item. These tests do not always deal with the 'failure' of a learner to do or learn something; they also encourage learners by pointing out to them where they have succeeded.

Unlike the placement test, the diagnostic test assesses very specific areas. For example, if a class has been taught the use of the relative clause without 'that', the teacher might want to know if the learner has learnt the item well. She/he will then administer a test. If the class has not learnt the item satisfactorily, the teacher can then plan a remedial lesson to re-teach the item.

ACHIEVEMENT (ATTAINMENT/SUMMATIVE) TESTS

These tests are the type all teachers and learners are familiar with. They can be administered by the teacher (class tests, school unit tests, half-yearly tests, etc.) or by an educational authority of the state or country (board examinations). Some school-leaving examinations, like the Cambridge examinations, test learner achievements throughout the world.

The achievement test looks over a longer period of time than, say, the diagnostic test, and it aims at finding out the standard which learners have reached in relation to other learners after instruction. It also discriminates between learners, placing them at different levels of achievement (Class I, II or III; Grade A, B or C; etc.). Since the learner's performance in achievement tests is considered a qualification, a lot of care must be taken in preparing the tests.

PROFICIENCY TESTS

These test the learner's ability to apply what she/he knows or has learnt to real situations. For example, if a person says that she/he knows how to speak Hindi, a proficiency test will set tasks which will require the person to speak, so that her/his proficiency in this area can be tested.

A proficiency test is not based upon any syllabus or teaching; it deals with the learner's real abilities at the time of taking the test. A proficiency test can be a pre-course test, and it is often used to assess the needs of learners. It is also used to design specific courses.

THINK IT OVER

1. What types of tests do we generally give our learners?
2. Is there a place for other types of tests in our curriculum?

Testing and teaching

Very often, testing and teaching are seen as two distinct areas of operation. In many places, the board of examinations sets question papers on the prescribed text independently, without really taking into account the type of teaching which has gone on. Ideally, teaching and testing should go together with neither being subservient to the other. The simple diagram on the right illustrates the relationship between teaching, testing and the educational objectives to be achieved.

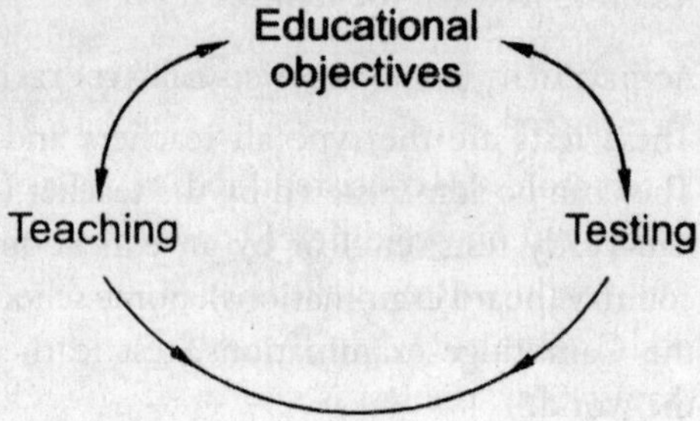

Educational objectives are spelt out by experts, and it is on the basis of these that the textbook is written and the teaching done. This in turn is evaluated. The feedback from testing is an assessment of how well the educational objectives have been realised.

Testing can affect teaching in another way. If the board of examination prepares a model test paper, all teaching will be geared towards making the learner competent to take the test. This is called the *backwash effect*. The backwash effect is a powerful tool and can influence teaching, and through teaching, the materials used in a classroom.

Characteristics of a good test

VALIDITY

A test which is ideal for measuring a particular type of language skill may be useless when it is used to measure some other skill. A test is valid when it measures what it sets out to measure. There are two types of validity:

- *Content validity:* This concerns what goes into a test. The content of a test should be finalised after deciding what is to be assessed and then specifying the content. This type of specification is known as content specification. The content specification makes clear the exact areas to be tested.

- *Face validity:* This concerns what learners and teachers think of the test. A test should look like a test. Face validity is not based on any scientific criterion, but it is important nevertheless. Very often learners and teachers reject tests which do not seem to be valid. Tests which use indirect ways of measuring abilities have a high rejection rate for reasons of face validity.

RELIABILITY

If test scores are consistent, that is, very nearly the same, when a group takes a test on two different days, the test is reliable. If a learner gets 65 per cent in writing skills when she/he takes the test on (say) Monday, and 67 per cent when she/he takes the test two or three days later on (say) Friday, the test is said to be reliable. On the other hand, if she/he gets 38 per cent on Monday and 56 per cent on Friday, the test is not reliable.

The 'instrument' used to measure a person's ability, namely, the test, must therefore be so constructed that it is reliable. One does not use a piece of elastic to measure a person's waist. One uses a tape measure, which does not stretch but remains the same.

PRACTICABILITY

This is the administrative aspect of testing. It deals with questions such as:

- Will the test require equipment such as a microphone and speaker?
- How long will the test take?
- Will the test cost too much to produce?
- Can it be easily printed or photocopied for the learners?

The other important factor is that of copying or cheating. A well-constructed test will take into account the possibility of malpractice. Since objective tests allow cheating easily, many competitive and qualifying examinations use different versions of the same test, thus reducing the possibility of malpractice in the examination hall.

COMPARISON AND DISCRIMINATION

A good test compares one learner with another, or a learner's earlier and later performances. The scores obtained by learners should also discriminate. If class 9 learners are given a class 6 test paper, all of them will score in the nineties. Such a test does not discriminate.

On the other hand, if class 9 learners are asked to take the IIT entrance examination, all of them will score poorly.

So, in order to discriminate, a test should be so constructed as to measure learner abilities at a particular stage. The ideal distribution of scores is a curve as shown in the figure. The larger number of scores generally cluster towards the middle (x).

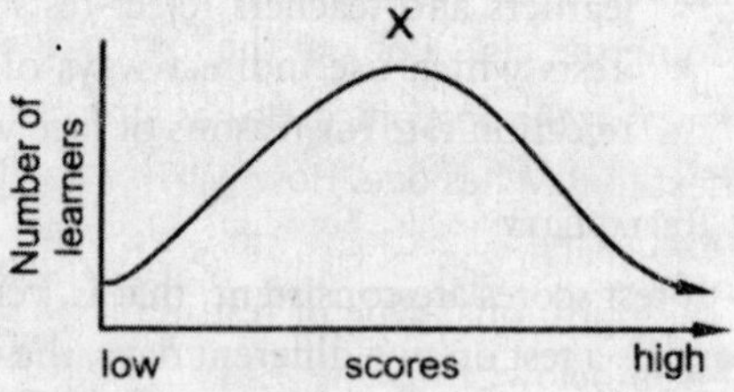

THINK IT OVER

1. Is any special training required to prepare tests?
2. Can a teacher learn to prepare good tests? Will it help the learners?

Test construction

Before a test is constructed, the following points have to be decided:

- What kind of test is this? (achievement, proficiency, diagnostic, placement)
- What should it measure? (reading or writing skills, speaking or listening skills, grammar or integrated skills)
- What sub-skills or abilities should it measure? (in reading, the ability to scan for information; in writing, the ability to use linking words like 'but', 'however' and 'nonetheless')
- What are the administrative constraints? (cost of printing the test; time available for correction, collating results, etc.)

The first step then is to write a set of specifications for the test, which will include all possible information on content, format, time in which the test must be taken, criteria for correction, and scoring procedures.

Content specification should deal with the lessons or the extent of syllabus to be covered. Format specification should deal with the question types, the number of questions, the time required for each question, breakup of marks, etc.

An important component of format specification is the *rubric.* Rubric is a set of instructions or explanations in an examination paper which tells one what to do. Economy and clarity should be the aim of all rubrics, but if the task so demands it, the rubric can run into a few lines. The rubric of a communicative task is generally lengthier as it has to give the content, the purpose of the task, and the procedure for doing the task. Look at the following example:

Ravi is at the post office. He has forgotten to bring his pen. A man standing next to Ravi has one. How will Ravi ask the man for the pen?

'Excuse me; ....'

The traditional type of test item, however, requires the sort of rubric given below:

Fill in the blank with the word or phrase that best completes the sentence.

Production of the test and marking specifications are administrative questions, but these very often influence the type of test paper which is prepared.

Often, different versions of a proficiency test are prepared to reduce the chances of malpractice in an examination hall. But production of such tests costs money in terms of paper and printing, so board examinations usually have one version of an examination paper, produced and stored under conditions of strict confidence.

Marking systems too vary according to the needs of the test. *Proficiency tests* (such as banking recruitment examinations) are generally objective as a large number of papers have to be corrected and the marking needs to be valid and reliable. On the other hand, *achievement tests* generally include a few questions where extended discourse is used. The marking, therefore, has an element of subjectivity. Much more thought needs to go into a question which has to be marked subjectively not only because its reliability and validity have to be considered, but also because questions regarding the time it will take to correct and whether the corrections can be standardised to some extent have to be dealt with.

Specifications for test construction can be summed up under the following heads:

Content (type of test)
Testees (population to be tested)
Topics (type of material to be used)

Operations

- Main skills
- Sub-skills

Format, including question types

Scoring/marking

APPLICATION

You have been asked to prepare a proficiency test in English for typists and stenographers. Write out the specifications in the format given above.

Types of testing items

OBJECTIVE-TYPE

These test items have only one right answer; so whoever corrects it at any time, the 'correct' answer will be the same. These items are preferred by many agencies like the UPSC and other recruitment boards as there can be no controversy about marking and the scores are both reliable and valid. The most common objective-type questions are discussed below.

Multiple-choice items

In the example below, the main sentence in the test item above is called the stem, and the four choices given are the distractors.

.... read R.K. Narayan's The English Teacher?

a. Did you
b. Have you
c. You will
d. You have

Multiple-choice questions seem easy to prepare, but in reality, it is very difficult to make a challenging item. The distractors must be plausible, and they must force the testee to look at the stem and make the right linguistic choice. Look at the following multiple-choice item.

From this passage, we learn that Adolf Hitler was ....

a. a French diplomat.
b. a German dictator.
c. an American president.
d. a Russian president.

This sort of a question can be answered even without looking at the distractors, because it is based on general knowledge and not on what the passage says. It is, therefore, a bad multiple-choice item.

Cloze items

This is a technique used to measure reading comprehension and general language ability. This procedure originated in the 1950s as a means of assessing the difficulty level of a reading passage for native speakers. In this test, each *n*th word is deleted, and the testee has to fill in the blank with the deleted item.

Under this item type, two types of scoring procedures are used: (1) the *exact word* method, where the exact word used in the original text must be supplied, and (2) the *appropriate* or *acceptable word* method, where the testee can supply any word which is acceptable or appropriate. Quite often, a cloze passage has provision for both the above scoring procedures, the exact words fitting into function gaps (conjunctions, prepositions and articles), and the appropriate words fitting into semantic gaps (nouns, adjectives, verbs, adverbs). See the following example from the *Longman Dictionary of Applied Linguistics* (1985):

A passage used in .... cloze test is a .... of written material in .... words have been regularly .... The subjects must then .... to reconstruct the passage .... filling in the missing ....

removed, a, by, try, passage, words, which

True/false items

Here, the information from a reading passage is paraphrased, and the testees have to judge whether the statement is true or false. This is one of the easiest of items to construct and score, and also an item which allows for a lot of guesswork.

Test constructors feel that a true/false item is good for teaching as it can be followed up by *why*-questions.

Why is it true?
Which part of the text tells you this?
Why is it false?

It may also be followed by:

Correct the false statements.

Gap-filling items

Unlike a multiple-choice item, no choices are given in a gap-filling item. Instead, the category of the words to be filled in (generally a structure or function word) is given. For example:

Complete the following using 'a', 'an', 'the' or the zero article.
Complete the following using suitable prepositions.

Information-transfer items

These items are generally based on a reading passage. The testee has to read the passage and complete a flow chart or table. Or, testees could be asked to read a passage and identify figures or diagrams. For example, they can be given a passage about types of doors, followed by drawings of different kinds of doors. They have to match the description to the pictures and identify them.

The input can sometimes be in the form of listening material. For example, in the test item below, testees listen to the description of a geographic region. They then complete the given key (in the image on the next page).

In this part of the test you will hear a description of land use in the South Kaula region. As you listen, you should decide what the symbols in the key below the map stand for. After this section of the test, you will be given time to complete the key. To do this, use the words in the box to the right of the key.

Joint Matriculation Board, March 1978

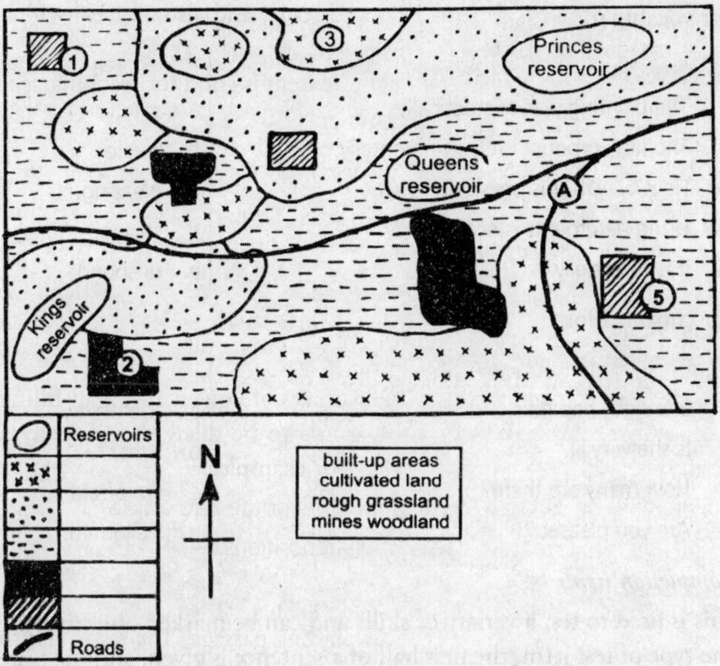

Matching items

These items cover grammar, vocabulary (meaning, collocation, connotation, etc.), or comprehension. They can be very simple or very challenging. For example:

For grammar

	A		B
1	If you mix blue and yellow	a	to join our group.
2	My grandfather, who is eighty,	b	you get green.
3	He is too young	c	that she danced round the room.
4	She was so happy	d	provided your application reaches us on time.
5	We will admit you in our college	e	walks five kilometres every day.

For vocabulary

	A		B
1	The painting was aesthetically	a	safe.
2	The new product is environmentally	b	viable.
3	He is wiry, but is physically	c	pleasing.
4	Using detergents is ecologically	d	strong.
5	It is financially	e	unsound.

For conversation

	A		B
1	She's got hepatitis.	a	Too many.
2	Is she very ill?	b	What?
3	How many are there?	c	I'm afraid so.
4	Are you pleased?	d	Delighted.

Completion items

This is used to test a variety of skills and can be marked objectively. In one type of test item, the first half of a sentence is given, and the testee completes it. Very often a clue is given in the form of another sentence. For example:

I didn't know about the party. I didn't come.
If I had ....

The man was deaf. He lectured on music.
The man who ....

In another type of item, clues or words and phrases are given, and the testee is asked to write a complete sentence. For example:

water – will not – supply – tomorrow
(Answer: Water will not be supplied tomorrow.)

Writing too can be tested using this type of item. For example, sets of words/phrases are given, and they must be put together to form a coherent letter. All features of language and discourse can be tested through this item.

SUBJECTIVE-TYPE

These are open-ended questions which test the learner's productive skills. There are three main types of items.

- Short answers: These are generally based on some text or given passage.
- Paragraph writing: These can be text-based or free.
- Essays, comments, and so on, on a given topic

The difference between the items consists in the amount of support given. For example, an open-ended writing item can read as follows:

Write an essay on 'Our transport system' in three hundred words.

or

Write an essay consisting of five paragraphs on 'Our transport system'.
The first paragraph should deal with transport in general.
The second should deal with land transport systems.
The third with water transport systems.
The fourth with air transport systems.
The last should conclude the essay.

The most important aspect of subjective-type questions is the preparation of marking criteria even *before* the item is prepared. The decision on what the item must test should be taken before writing the item. A paragraph, for example, has many features, ranging from spelling and handwriting to discourse features like the use of linkers, vocabulary and various sentence structures. What is to be given greater weightage should be clear, otherwise the scoring becomes arbitrary.

Speaking is another area where subjective scoring is done. But here again, if the criteria for marking are worked into the scheme of the examination, there is more consistency in scoring. One examiner might want to know whether the testee can speak fluently on professional topics, while another might want to know the general fluency level of the testee—whether his/her speech is fragmentary or only occasionally hesitant.

SECTION SUMMARY

- Testing is the means of measuring ability, knowledge or performance.

- There are four main types of tests: placement, diagnostic, achievement and proficiency.
- Tests can be either forward-looking (related to the future of the testee) or backward-looking (related to what the testee has done in the past).
- Testing and teaching are closely linked, and one can influence the other, either positively or negatively.
- The main characteristics of a good test are validity, reliability and practicability—a good test should compare and discriminate.
- Test construction should consider the syllabus/content to be tested, the learners who are to be tested, the objectives of the test, the types of items to be included, the format, and the marking scheme.
- Two main types of test items are objective test items and subjective (or open-ended) items.

Did you understand?

1. Given below are different types of tests. Say whether they are forward-looking or backward-looking or both.
   a. Placement
   b. Achievement
   c. Diagnostic
   d. Proficiency
2. What is validity? How many types of validity are there?
3. How does one know that a test is reliable? What are the characteristics of a reliable test?
4. How are teaching and testing connected?
5. Write short notes on:
   a. Backwash effect
   b. Multiple-choice questions
   c. Scoring tests

Application

Task 1

On the next page are some instructions and tasks. Study them. Are the tasks clear? Can they be understood easily by learners of class 9? Suggest changes, if necessary.

a. Fill in the missing words in the following sentences by combining the verb in capital letters with a suitable adverb particle (out, under, down, up, in)
   He was very ………… when his dog was run over by a car. (SET)
b. Choose the word that best matches the meaning of the word in the sentence.
   Ramani's parents persuaded her to try again.
   i. pressed iii. punished
   ii. convinced iv. compelled
c. Study the following pairs of sentences and answer the questions that follow:
   Anil cut his finger. Alam cut off his finger.
   Question: Which boy has lost his finger?

TASK 2

Study the multiple-choice questions and decide what each is testing. Comment on the distractors. Can you improve the items?

a. She wanted to go prepared to Ooty, so she bought an ………… .
   i. blanket iii. umbrella
   ii. toaster iv. coat
b. ………… the ones who know the answers.
   i. They are iii. They're
   ii. There iv. Their

TASK 3

Can you improve the test item below?

Put the following sentences in the right order and write two paragraphs on 'Eagles'. You can add or delete sentences or change them. You can indicate what the first sentence is. Check an encyclopaedia about facts before making any changes in the content.

Eagles

The osprey is found in Australia, Africa and Europe.
They have very good eyesight.
Eagles live in many parts of the world.
It usually builds its nest up in a tree.
They fly high in the sky until they see a small animal.
A common Asian eagle is the osprey.

Then they dive down suddenly and catch it.
The osprey lives on fish.
Some eagles grow up to one metre long.
It is dark brown above and white below.
It often catches quite heavy fish.
Other eagles such as the kestrel live on mice, small animals and birds.

TASK 4

Given below is the blueprint of the Andhra Pradesh SSC examination third-language English paper.

SSC Examination Andhra Pradesh Third-Language English
Design of Papers I and II

Paper	Skill / objective	Content area	Qn. type	No. of qns.	Marks	Qn. nos.
IA	Recall of content	Reader Prose	SA	5	10	1–5
		Reader Poetry	Quote	1	2	7
	Reading Comprehension	Reader Poetry	SA	1	3	6
		Reader Prose	SA	2	5	8, 9
IB	Language	Structure	SA	7	10	10–16
		Vocabulary	VSA	5	10	17–21
		Spelling Dictionary	SA	4	4	22–25
		Skills	SA	1	2	26
		Functions and use	SA	4	4	27–30
IIA	Recall of content	Suppl. Reader	SA	5	5	1–5
	Reading Comprehension	Suppl. Reader	SA	1	5	6
	Writing	Narration/ Description	E	1	10	7
		Letter	E	1	10	8

IIB	Reading Comprehension	Workbook	SA	1	5	9
		Unseen	OT			
		Passages	SA	2	15	10, 11

E: essay; SA: short answer; VSA: very short answer (one or two words, or a phrase); OT: out of text

Using the design, prepare a question paper based on a class 8 or class 9 textbook. Try to see that you include as many question types as possible. Work in groups. After you have completed your paper, exchange it with other groups. Give critical comments.

TASK 5

Given below is the breakup of objectives/skills and content area of a test and the weightage. Study it and answer the questions that follow.

OBJECTIVES/SKILLS	
Reading comprehension	30%
Content of prescribed readers	10%
Writing	20%
Language	40%
CONTENT AREAS	
Reader	10%
Language	40%
Supplementary reader	10%
Writing	20%
Unfamiliar/unseen passage	20%

a. What areas do you think the teacher will concentrate on while teaching in the class?
b. What type of book will be prescribed?
c. Can you indicate the type of test the learners will be given?

Proficiency tests

The rise of English as a global language has been followed by a rise in the number of proficiency tests in English. Multinational companies, institutes of higher education, the medical profession, and others now demand a valid certification of one's proficiency level in English, before the candidate gets a job or is admitted to a course.

The Test of English as a Foreign Language (TOEFL), conducted by the Education Testing Services of America, has been the premier proficiency test for gaining admission to universities in the USA for many years. In the UK, the International English Language Testing System (IELTS) developed by Cambridge University has been recognised as a certifying examination of proficiency in English not only for higher studies, but also for emigration to Commonwealth countries, such as Canada, New Zealand and Australia.

Earlier, proficiency tests were taken almost exclusively by candidates who wished to study or work abroad. But today, international English proficiency examinations are being taken by students and employees who do not have plans to go abroad, but whose parents, teachers or employers want to know the level of their proficiency.

The direct result of the increase in demand for proficiency tests in English in non-English-speaking countries has been rigorous standardisation. Here, the Council of Europe's Common European Framework has come in very useful for deciding levels of proficiency in English. In fact, almost all bodies that offer language proficiency tests in the UK and in Europe, as well as in Australia and New Zealand, follow the CEF to a greater or lesser degree.

The other result has been the introduction of principles of criterion-referenced testing by developers of this examination. Grades not marks, bands not points, are used to describe the proficiency levels of the candidates. An example of the bands used to evaluate candidates in IELTS is given below.

IELTS band descriptors

Band 9: Expert user

The test taker has fully operational command of the language. Their use of English is appropriate, accurate and fluent, and shows complete understanding.

Band 8: Very good user
The test taker has fully operational command of the language with only occasional unsystematic inaccuracies and inappropriate usage. They may misunderstand some things in unfamiliar situations. They handle complex and detailed argumentation well.

Band 7: Good user
The test taker has operational command of the language, though with occasional inaccuracies, inappropriate usage and misunderstandings in some situations. They generally handle complex language well and understand detailed reasoning.

Band 6: Competent user
The test taker has an effective command of the language despite some inaccuracies, inappropriate usage and misunderstandings. They can use and understand fairly complex language, particularly in familiar situations.

Band 5: Modest user
The test taker has a partial command of the language and copes with overall meaning in most situations, although they are likely to make many mistakes. They should be able to handle basic communication in their own field.

Band 4: Limited user
The test taker's basic competence is limited to familiar situations. They frequently show problems in understanding and expression. They are not able to use complex language.

Band 3: Extremely limited user
The test taker conveys and understands only general meaning in very familiar situations. There are frequent breakdowns in communication.

Band 2: Intermittent user
The test taker has great difficulty understanding spoken and written English.

Band 1: Non-user
The test taker has no ability to use the language except a few isolated words.

Band 0: Did not attempt the test
The test taker did not answer the questions.

ielts.org

The IELTS test assesses abilities in listening, reading, writing and speaking. The test format for each skill involves multiple tasks. For example, the writing test requires test takers to complete two tasks. Each of these tasks is assessed with regard to task achievement, coherence and cohesion, lexical resource, and grammatical range and accuracy. Some of the assessment criteria for the first writing task of the IELTS General Training[1] examination are shown in the tables on pages 219–220. Simple and clear criteria such as these helps all stakeholders better understand the level of performance required to secure a particular band score.

A further characteristic of these proficiency tests is the sort of specialisation that is gradually coming in. There are tests to evaluate specific skills: reading, writing, listening and speaking. The Graded Examinations in Spoken English (GESE) of the Trinity Examinations Board, as its name suggests, is a proficiency test of only spoken English. Other tests evaluate how well the candidates communicate at the workplace. Business English Certificate (BEC) is one such examination. Similarly, there are examinations to check a healthcare worker's proficiency in English at the workplace. The Occupational English Test (OET) is administered to pharmacists, radiologists, nurses, dentists and other persons in the medical field who wish to work in Australia. The Pearson Test of English (Academic) uses artificial intelligence to deliver and evaluate a proficiency test. Candidates do the tasks on a computer, and the correction is done without human intervention (in essence, the machine does the evaluation based on the data it has been fed). This test is popular with students seeking admission in foreign universities.

[1] There are two IELTS examinations available: IELTS Academic measures whether the testee's English language level is suitable for an academic environment, while IELTS General Training measures English language proficiency in the practical, everyday context of the workplace and social situations.

Band	Task achievement	Coherence and cohesion	Lexical resource	Grammatical range and accuracy
9	• fully satisfies all the requirements of the task • clearly presents a fully developed response	• uses cohesion in such a way that it attracts no attention • skilfully manages paragraphing	• uses a wide range of vocabulary with very natural and sophisticated control of lexical features; rare minor errors occur only as 'slips'	• uses a wide range of structures with full flexibility and accuracy; rare minor errors occur only as 'slips'
6	• addresses the requirements of the task • presents a purpose that is generally clear; there may be inconsistencies in tone • presents and adequately highlights key features/ bullet points but details may be irrelevant, inappropriate or inaccurate	• arranges information and ideas coherently and there is a clear overall progression • uses cohesive devices effectively, but cohesion within and/or between sentences may be faulty or mechanical • may not always use referencing clearly or appropriately	• uses an adequate range of vocabulary for the task • attempts to use less common vocabulary but with some inaccuracy • makes some errors in spelling and/or word formation, but they do not impede communication	• uses a mix of simple and complex sentence forms • makes some errors in grammar and punctuation but they rarely reduce communication

ielts.org

Band	Task achievement	Coherence and cohesion	Lexical resource	Grammatical range and accuracy
4	• attempts to address the task but does not cover all key features/bullet points; the format may be inappropriate • fails to clearly explain the purpose of the letter; the tone may be inappropriate • may confuse key features/ bullet points with detail; parts may be unclear, irrelevant, repetitive or inaccurate	• presents information and ideas but these are not arranged coherently and there is no clear progression in the response • uses some basic cohesive devices but these may be inaccurate or repetitive	• uses only basic vocabulary which may be used repetitively or which may be inappropriate for the task • has limited control of word formation and/or spelling; • errors may cause strain for the reader	• uses only a very limited range of structures with only rare use of subordinate clauses • some structures are accurate but errors predominate, and punctuation is often faulty
2	• answer is barely related to the task	• has very little control of organisational features	• uses an extremely limited range of vocabulary; essentially no control of word formation and/or spelling	• cannot use sentence forms except in memorised phrases

ielts.org

Since the computer and the internet are very much a part of the classroom and the workplace, many proficiency tests make use of this facility and offer tests online. Test results and comments are also generated online, and are almost instantaneous.

The most significant point to note, however, is the fact that these tests are not looking for 'native speaker' characteristics in speech or interaction. They are evaluating the candidate against a truly 'international' norm that reflects the reality of English in the world. The quote below from a brochure of Trinity College London from a few years ago neatly sums up the main features of proficiency tests in English.

> From Trinity's headquarters in London, we deliver examinations in over fifty countries worldwide. We accept all varieties of the English language, we encourage cultural variety in performance. At the same time we apply global standards to ensure that our examinations carry the same weight wherever and whenever they are taken.

In India, too, authorities and ELT bodies have developed proficiency tests in English. Test items are developed by ELT experts, and teachers and ELT professionals are trained as examiners. These exams are offered to customers all over India. Some bodies also prepare proficiency tests that would perhaps be taken by a limited clientele. The National Test of Proficiency in Spoken English, developed by the English Language Teachers Association of India (ELTAI), based in Chennai, was an example of such an initiative.

The most important factors for a proficiency test to be 'successful' are (a) the test should be valid (it should test what it says it tests) and reliable (wherever and whenever it is administered), and (b) it should have accreditation. Most international tests of proficiency fulfil both these criteria.

SECTION SUMMARY

- More and more people today want to find out how proficient employees/students are in English. This is because English has become a global language.
- Proficiency tests in English assess both general proficiency as well as proficiency required in specific fields of work/study.
- Initiatives have been taken in India to develop proficiency tests in English.

Did you understand?

1. Name some proficiency tests in English that are available in India today.
2. Can you name two proficiency tests that focus on 'special' areas?
3. What are the main characteristics of proficiency tests that are available today?

Application

Task 1

List three skills each of reading and writing that a student should have mastered at the end of class 10.

Task 2

Devise global band descriptors for writing at three levels (Band 1 being the lowest and Band 3 being the highest).

Writing

Band 1: ....

Band 2: ....

Band 3: ....

Task 3

Given below are a task and the responses of two class 10 students. What band would you award these candidates? Explain your reasons.

> Write a story entitled 'The empty house' in 100 words.
>
> Script A
>
> This house is a old mansion. You can find no one there living. It is far from the town and it is a haunted house. The house is full empty there is nothing inside. I saw this when a murder had been done when a person entered the house alone and police are investigating. They couldn't find any clue. Then they told it is dangerous to be here or to go there so everybody better go home. I was really scared. As soon as the Police locked the door we heard a sound of a footsteps inside and something feel even though the house was empty. From that day it is left just like that and no one goes there even now.
>
> No. of words: 122

Script B

One March 1st I went to the park for a walk, the area was new to me because we had just shifted in. While walking I spotted a house. A huge house! I was tempted at once. I walked to the house when I went to knock on the door I saw the knob broken. I immedetly walked in, when I walked in I could see nothing except for cob webs it was as though no one had entered the house for years together.

I roamed almost half of the house until I got lost. I had panicked a lot luckily a man from the street saw the door opened and asked 'Is anyone there' I shouted 'help' 'help' he than came in and searched for me. He found me and led me out of the house. I thanked him a lot and went running back home. After that day I never entered anyone's house again.

No. of words: 156

Useful Books

Grammar

- *Help with Grammar* (Books 1 and 2), W. Forsyth and S. Lavender: Viva Books
- *Help with Phrasal Verbs*, R. Acklam: Viva Books

  These books are useful for quick reference and have a variety of exercises that can be used either to teach students or for self-study.
- *A Teacher's Grammar of English*, K.R. Narayanaswamy: Orient BlackSwan

  This book deals with the 'grammar' of both the written and spoken forms of English. It also focuses on the communicative aspect of each of the grammatical categories it deals with.
- *Advanced Grammar in Use* (with answers), M. Hewing: Cambridge University Press (CLPE)[1]

  As advanced users of English, we often have doubts about some usage aspects. This book tries to address most of these problem areas. It has, in addition, a basic grammar reference section.
- *Grammar Practice Activities*, P. Ur: Cambridge University Press (CLPE)

  This book has a collection of grammar activities that are communicative in nature. The activities can be used as they are, or can be easily adapted to suit the requirements of different classroom situations.
- *English Grammar in Use* (Elementary and Intermediate), R. Murphy: Cambridge University Press

[1] Cambridge Low-Priced Edition

The two grammar books by Murphy can be used by teachers as reference books on usage points and also as a resource for preparing grammar exercises.

Teacher's resource books

- *The Resourceful English Teacher*, J. Chandler and M. Stone: Viva Books
  This book contains a collection of classroom activities using various resources such as newspapers, radio, etc.
- *Five-Minute Activities*, P. Ur and A. Wright: Cambridge University Press (CLPE)
  This book has over 120 ideas for language activities in the classroom. These activities can be used in classrooms at many levels. The activities can act as 'fillers' or even warm-up exercises.
- *Fun and Games in English*, C. Chaves and A. Graham: Viva Books
  This has a number of games and activities that can be used as they are, or adapted by the teacher to suit the class.

English language teaching methodology

- *English Language Teaching: Principles and Practice*, V. Saraswati: Orient BlackSwan
  This is an ELT manual written from a very Indian perspective. Useful for teachers of English, BEd students and teacher trainers.
- *The Language Curriculum. Dynamics of Change* (Volumes 1 and 2), eds. R. Mathew, L. Eapen and J. Tharu: Orient BlackSwan
  Volume 1 deals mainly with classroom activities, curriculum preparation and evaluation; Volume 2 centres on the teacher in India and presents a lot of ethnographic information.
- *Readings in English Language Teaching in India*, ed. S. Kudchedkar: Orient BlackSwan
  Various aspects of ELT are debated and discussed in this book of essays. Useful for BEd trainees, ELT trainers and ELT specialists.
- *Teaching and Learning English: A Sourcebook for Teachers and Teacher-Trainers*, M.L. Tickoo: Orient BlackSwan
  This is a reference book that would be useful, as the title suggests, for ELT teacher trainers as well as students of ELT.

- *Approaches and Methods to Language Teaching*, J.C. Richards and T.S. Rodgers: Cambridge University Press (CLPE)
  This classic book on ELT methodology is a useful reference book for all teachers and trainers involved in teacher training/ specialisation in ELT.

Spoken English and phonetics

- *Better English Pronunciation*, J.D. O'Connor: Cambridge University Press (CLPE)
  Another essential book for any teacher interested in aspects of spoken English. Along with phonetic description of sounds, stress and intonation, this book has a variety of useful exercises. Also available as an audio CD.
- *English Pronouncing Dictionary* (18th Edition), D. Jones, et al.: Cambridge University Press
  A reference book that is useful for teachers and teacher trainers, it helps one to check the pronunciation of words. This is a tool teachers can use while making lesson plans or preparing a reading passage.
- *English Phonetics and Phonology*, P. Roach: Cambridge University Press (CLPE)
  This is a comprehensive text on phonetics and it deals with spoken English features with regard to not just Standard English but other varieties too. This would be of interest to students of phonetics or people interested in the formal aspects of phonetics. Suitable for advanced learners.

Dictionaries

All major publishing houses, such as Oxford University Press, Macmillan, Cambridge University Press, and Orient BlackSwan, have published learner's dictionaries at various levels. Most dictionaries are accompanied by CDs, which have a lot of supplementary material such as usage points and tips for writing. Some CDs are interactive, that is, the user's voice can be recorded and later replayed. The choice of the dictionary would depend on the requirements of the target group.

Glossary of ELT Terms

acceptable Acceptable English is English that can be understood by the listener/hearer. Acceptable here does not necessarily mean 'faultless'; a speaker can make mistakes as long as the message is conveyed. Acceptable English does not cause offence to the listener. Unacceptable English does not convey the meaning and can cause offence.

accuracy The capacity of a learner to produce grammatically correct sentences. This may not include the ability to speak or write FLUENTLY, or use sentences APPROPRIATE to the situation.

applied linguistics The study of language and linguistics in relation to the practical aspects of teaching/learning a language, usually a foreign or second language.

appropriacy | appropriateness | appropriate The knowledge of the user of a language regarding what is suitable for a particular situation.

authentic Texts/excerpts from newspapers, magazines, books, etc., which have not been primarily written for English language teaching purposes.

bilingual A person who knows and uses two languages equally well.

body language The use of facial expressions, body posture and movements to communicate MEANING. (See PARALINGUISTIC FEATURES.)

choral repetition | chorus repetition A class repeats an example/sentence given by the teacher, as one group.

chunk The division of spoken or written language into smaller sections, done to help a learner comprehend what is said or written. For example, a paragraph can be divided into meaningful units to help learners to understand. Or, a speech can be broken up into sections.

cloze test Every *n*th word is removed and the testee has to guess the most appropriate word that can be used in the blank spaces.

collocation The way in which words are used together regularly.

communication skills The skills possessed by a user of a language for sending and receiving messages. In language teaching, this refers to verbal skills.

competency A person's ability to create and understand sentences, including those they have never heard before.

corpus A collection of spoken or written material, often in machine readable form.

correct A word which is used to judge whether a particular language usage is right or wrong.

cue A signal given by a teacher to elicit a response from the student. A cue can be words or pictures.

descriptive grammar A grammar which describes how a language is actually spoken/written. (See PRESCRIPTIVE GRAMMAR.)

dialogue A model conversation used to practise speaking. Dialogues can focus on particular grammar or vocabulary items.

discriminate | discrimination The degree to which a TEST or test item distinguishes between better and weaker students.

elicitation The technique used by a teacher to get learners to produce speech or writing.

English as a Foreign Language (EFL) English taught as a subject and not used as a medium of instruction or as a means of communication within the country.

English as a Second Language (ESL) English used for communication within the country as well as a medium of instruction in schools/universities. Sometimes the language is used by the government too.

error An imperfect production of language caused by incomplete or faulty learning. A mistake, on the other hand, is caused by lack of attention, carelessness, fatigue, etc. Mistakes are related to performance.

exponent The actual language used to express a function or notion.

extensive reading Reading widely and in quantity to get a GIST or general understanding of what one is reading. Extensive reading is done to develop good reading habits and build up knowledge of vocabulary, structure, style etc. (See INTENSIVE READING.)

filler Hesitation while speaking filled by *er*, *umm*, *ah*, *you know*, etc.

first language The language which is being taught in a formal setting, such as that in a school.

fluency | fluent Speech which has the quality of being natural and normal, not forced and artificial. When English is taught/learnt, the objective usually is to acquire fluency along with ACCURACY in the target language.

form The way an element of language is expressed in speech or writing; thus, written and spoken forms.

function The purpose for which a particular bit of language is used; the same FORM may be used for different functions (for example, the imperative for orders, requests and instructions).

gist The general idea or MEANING that a reader or a listener gathers.

hardware The equipment, usually electrical, found in classrooms. For example, cassette player, computer, overhead projector, etc.

information gap In a communicative activity, when information is known only to some and not others. Information gap promotes real language use.

information transfer An activity in which learners identify relevant information from a reading or listening text and reproduce it in diagrammatic form—or vice versa.

integrated approach | integration of skills In language teaching, LSRW skills are not presented/practised in isolation. Activities encourage using two or more skills in conjunction.

intensive reading Reading usually done at a slower speed and with limited reading material. The purpose of intensive reading is total comprehension. Academic reading is usually intensive reading.

interference | mother-tongue interference The use of mother-tongue language patterns to produce the target language, leading to ERRORS.

key words The most important words that carry the MEANING of the sentence.

lexical set A group of words that have in common MEANING, situation, subject matter, etc. They are also called word families.

literacy The ability to read and write a language. Functional literacy refers to the minimum level of reading and writing required to function effectively in a job.

lockstep Classroom management where the teacher is in total control and where only one interaction takes place at a time.

meaning What the language expresses about the world we live in or any other imaginary world.

meaningful drill One in which the degree of control over the response is not totally teacher-controlled. The learner has the freedom to choose from many responses.

mechanical drill The learner's response is totally controlled. Comprehension of the item by the learner is not required.

meta-language Language used to talk about language; for example, grammar words like verb, adjective, noun.

motivation That which determines a person's desire to learn a new language.

notions Concepts and MEANINGS the learner needs in order to communicate.

paralinguistic features Non-vocal phenomena, such as facial expressions, eye movements, gestures, etc. (See BODY LANGUAGE.)

performance How a person actually uses the language. A person's knowledge of the language is called COMPETENCE and how the person uses this knowledge to produce and understand language is performance.

phonics A method by which children are taught to recognise relationships between letters and sounds.

prescriptive grammar A grammar which states rules for what it considers the most CORRECT usage. It is not based on how a language is actually used, but on how the grammarian thinks it *should* be used.

procedure Techniques used in the classroom to achieve objectives.

rapport Friendly positive relationship established between the teacher and the class. Classes work well and students learn better if there is rapport between the teacher and the class.

realia Real objects and things brought into the class as aids. Used to illustrate MEANINGS more clearly, clarify concepts, make a situation more meaningful, etc.

redundancy Spoken or written language that contains more information than necessary to convey a message or for comprehension. Technical/scientific writing is difficult to read because there is very little redundancy there. Almost 50% of normal language is said to be redundant.

register Type of speech used by a group of people usually in the same profession (e.g., doctors, lawyers) or sharing the same interests (e.g., coin collectors, cricket fans).

reinforcement The response to a STIMULUS can be strengthened or weakened as desired. This is called positive reinforcement and negative reinforcement.

role playing Drama-like activity in which learners take different roles in a typical situation. This technique is used to give learners practice in how to use language in different situations.

scales A range of values forming a system for measuring or grading.

speech community A group of people who form a community and who have at least one speech variety in common.

stimulus That which produces a change or reaction. A stimulus evokes a response.

task Used in communicative language teaching, a task requires a learner to process and understand the language to complete it successfully.

test A TASK that students are required to perform, usually unaided, to show what they know and do not know.

utterance Something that is spoken; usually short, as one part of a dialogue. An exchange is made up of many utterances.

References

Abbott, G. and P. Wingard, eds. 1981. *The teaching of English as an international language*. London: Collins.

Alderson, J.C. and A. Urquhart, eds. 1984. *Reading in a foreign language*. London: Longman.

Allen, J.P.B. 1980. 'A three-level curriculum model for second-language education'. Modern Language Centre, Ontario Institute for Studies in Education (mimeo).

Allen, V.F. 1983. 'Reasons for the present emphasis on vocabulary'. In *Techniques in teaching vocabulary*. Oxford: Oxford University Press.

Anthony, E.M. 1972. 'Approach, method and technique'. In *Teaching English as a second language*, edited by H.B. Allen and R.N. Campbell. New York: McGraw-Hill.

Bagchi, G. 1985. Talk at the RIE, Singapore. Not published.

Berman, M. 1981. *Playing and working with words*. Oxford: Pergamon Press.

Billows, F.L. 1961. *The techniques of language teaching*. London: Longman.

Brook-Hart, G. 2004. *Instant IELTS*. Cambridge: Cambridge University Press.

Brumfit, C.J. 1980a. 'From defining to designing: communicative specifications versus communicative methodology in foreign language teaching'. In *The foreign language syllabus and communicative approaches to teaching: Proceedings of a European–American seminar*, edited by K.E. Müller. Special issue of *Studies in second language acquisition*.

__________. 1980b. *Problems and principles of English language teaching*. Oxford: Oxford University Press.

________. 1982. 'Humanistic approaches: An empirical view'. *ELT documents* 113. The British Council.

Brumfit, C.J. and K. Johnson, eds. 1979. *The communicative approach to language teaching*. Oxford: Oxford University Press.

Candlin, C.N., ed. 1981. *The communicative teaching of English: Principles and an exercise typology*. London: Longman.

Chaplen, F. 1970. *Paragraph writing*. London: Alden E. Mawbray.

Coleman, A. 1929. *The teaching of modern foreign languages in the United States* (referred to as the Coleman Report).

Crystal, D. 1997. *English as a global language*. Cambridge: Cambridge University Press.

Culshaw, C. and D. Waters. 1984. *Headwork 4*. Oxford: Oxford University Press.

Dangerfield, L. 1985. 'Island: An integrated skills activity'. In *At the chalkface*, edited by A. Matthews, M. Spratt and L. Dangerfield. London: Edward Arnold.

Dodson, C.J. 1967. *Language teaching and the bilingual method*. London: Pitman.

Doff, A. 1988. *Teach English: A training course for teachers*. Cambridge University Press in association with the British Council.

Edge, J. 1993. *Essentials of English language teaching*. CCL Corporation.

Freeman, S. 1977. *Written communication in English*. Mumbai: Orient Longman.

Freire, P. 1972. *Pedagogy of the oppressed*. London: Penguin.

French, F.G. 1960. *English in tables*. London: Oxford University Press.

Frisby, A.W. 1957. *Teaching English*. London: Longman.

Gatenby, E.V. 1958. *A direct method English course: Book I*. London: Longman, Green & Co.

Graddol, D. 1997. *The future of English?* London: The British Council.

________. 2006. *English next*. London: The British Council.

Graham, C. 1979. *Jazz chants for children*. New York: Oxford University Press.

Gurrey, P. 1955. *Teaching English as a foreign language*. London: Longmans, Green.

Harmer, J. 1983. *The practice of English language teaching*. Essex: Longman.

Harrison, A. 1983. *A language testing handbook*. London: Macmillan.

Heaton, J.B., ed. 1982. *Language testing*. London: Macmillan Education.

Howatt, A.P.R. 1984. *A history of English language teaching*. Oxford: Oxford University Press.

Hubbard, P., H. Jones, B. Thornton and R. Wheeler. 1983. *A training course for TEFL*. Oxford: Oxford University Press.

Hughes, A. 1989. *Testing for language teachers*. Cambridge: Cambridge University Press.

Hughes, G.S. 1981. *A handbook of classroom English*. Oxford: Oxford University Press.

Johnson, K. and K. Morrow, eds. 1981. *Communication in the classroom*. London: Longman.

Johnson, T.D. and D.R. Louis. 1985. *Literacy through literature*. Sydney: Methuen.

Kachru, B. 1985. 'Standards, codification and sociolinguistic realism: The English language in the outer circle'. In *English in the world: Teaching and learning the language and literatures,* edited by R. Quirk and H.G. Widdowson. Cambridge: Cambridge University Press.

Krashen, S.D. 1981. *Second language acquisition and second language learning*. Oxford: Pergamon Press.

Larsen-Freeman, D. 1986. *Techniques and principles in language teaching*. Oxford: Oxford University Press.

Lee, W.R. 1979. *Language teaching games and contests*. Oxford: Oxford University Press.

Lewis, M. 1997. *Implementing the lexical approach: Putting theory into practice*. Hove: Language Teaching Publications.

Littlewood, W. 1981. *Communicative language teaching*. New York: Cambridge University Press.

Longman dictionary of applied linguistics. 1985.

Longman dictionary of contemporary English. 1978.

Mackey, W.F. 1965. *Language teaching analysis*. London: Longman.

Maley, A. 1984. '"I got religion!": Evangelism in language teaching'. In *Initiatives in communicative language teaching*, edited by S. Savignon and M.S. Berns. Reading: Addison-Wesley.

Matthews, A., M. Spratt and L. Dangerfield, eds. 1985. *At the chalkface*. London: Edward Arnold.

Morrow, K. 1981. 'Principles of communicative methodology'. In *Communication in the classroom*, edited by K. Johnson and K. Morrow. London: Longman.

Moulton, W. 1961. 'Linguistics and language teaching in the United States, 1940–60'. In *Trends in European and American linguistics 1930–1960*, edited by C. Mohrmann, A. Sommerfelt and J. Whatmough. Utrecht: Spectrum Publishers.

Mugglestone, P. 1980. *Planning and using the blackboard*. London: Allen & Unwin.

Orwell, G. 1945. *Animal farm*. London: Martin Secker & Warburg Ltd.

________. 1965. *Decline of the English murder and other essays*. London: Penguin Books with Secker & Warburg Ltd.

Patel, M.S. 1962. 'The structural syllabus at work in India'. *ELT Journal* XVI (3): 145–51.

Pittman, G.A. 1967. *Teaching structural English*, rev. edn. London: Ginn & Co. Ltd.

Prabhu, N.S. 1987. *Second language pedagogy*. Oxford: Oxford University Press.

Raimes, A. 1983. *Techniques in teaching writing*. New York: Oxford University Press.

Rea-Dickins, P. and K. Germaine. 1992. *Evaluation*. Oxford: Oxford University Press.

Read, C. 1985. 'Integrating the skills'. In *At the chalkface*, edited by A. Matthews, M. Spratt and L. Dangerfield. London: Edward Arnold.

Richards, H. 1981. 'Doctor Goldsmith's medicine'. In *Junior English 3*, rev. edn. London: Ginn & Co. Ltd.

Rivers, W.M. 1964. *The psychologist and the foreign-language teacher*. Chicago and London: University of Chicago Press.

__________. 1968. *Teaching foreign-language skills*. Chicago: University of Chicago Press.

__________. 1983. *Communicating naturally in a second language*. Cambridge: Cambridge University Press.

Rivers, W.M. and M.S. Temperley. 1978. *A practical guide to the teaching of English*. Oxford: Oxford University Press.

Rixon, S. 1981. *How to use games in language teaching*. London: Macmillan.

Seaton, B. 1982. *A handbook of English language teaching terms and practice*. London: Macmillan.

Stern, H.H. 1983. *Fundamental concepts of language teaching*. Oxford: Oxford University Press.

Stevick, E.W. 1990. *Humanism in language teaching: A critical perspective*. Oxford: Oxford University Press.

Sweet, H. 1964. *The practical study of languages*. Oxford: Oxford University Press.

Tickoo, M.L. 1988. 'Introducing Michael Philip West'. In *A centenary tribute to Michael Philip West*, edited by Velayudhan. RIE, Singapore Publication.

Tolstoy, L. 1862. 'Training and education'. In *Tolstoy on education*, edited by A. Pinch and M. Armstrong. 1982. Athlone Press.

Trim, J.L.M. 1981. 'Résumé'. In *Modern languages (1971–1981): Report presented by CDCC project group 4*. Strasbourg: Council of Europe Publishing.

Widdowson, H.G. 1978. *Teaching language as communication*. Oxford: Oxford University Press.

Wilkins, D.A. 1976. *Notional syllabuses*. Oxford: Oxford University Press.

Willis, J. 1981. *Teaching English through English*. London: Longman.

Wingard, P. 1981. 'Audio-visual aids for teaching English'. In *The teaching of English as an international language*, edited by G. Abbott and P. Wingard. London: Collins.

Wright, A., D. Betteridge and M. Buckby. 1984. *Games for language learning*. Cambridge: Cambridge University Press.

Yalden, J. 1983. *The communicative syllabus: Evolution, design and implementation*. Oxford: Pergamon Press.

Index